Let go MOM

.........I WILL BE FINE

Let go MOM

.........I WILL BE FINE

Shivi Dua

Wisdom Village Publications Pvt Ltd

Knowledge is information. Wisdom is transformation.

A WISDOM VILLAGE PRESENTATION

Books from Wisdom Village Publications envision to enhance and enrich their readers with life changing experiences from the business, mind, body and soul genres. They strive towards holistic development.

Editing : Renuka Sagar

ISBN 978 93 80710259

Published in 2012 by:

Wisdom Village Publications Pvt Ltd

Knowledge is information. Wisdom is transformation.

www.wisdomvillagepublications.com

To Book Your Orders:

Email: wvpdindia@gmail.com

Or Call: +91 9810800469

Published by Anu Anand for Wisdom Village;

Cover Design and Page Setting by Sunil Mathur;

Printed at Thomson Press (India) Ltd.

Preface

It has been a well known fact since ages that there is divinity in motherhood: Just like the Creator created us, loves and nurtures us, so does the mother. He is there for us unconditionally, and so is the mother there for her children. Then why would a book on motherhood make any sense? Each mother is the supreme for her child. Can any book teach anyone anything about motherhood? Can even a mother teach any other mother about motherhood? The answer probably is no, because in any case a mother gives her best to her children. What more can anyone do anyway?

Yet, a mother is a human being, too. A human being is prone to making mistakes because that is where she learns from and evolves. Anyone willing to learn will find a lot in the universe to learn from and improve upon oneself, even a mother. Motherhood, no doubt, is a divine gift but having received the gift, a mother applies all her human skills to do her best for her child – nourishing, nurturing, protecting, teaching and guiding her child, the best way that she can. Very often it happens that while protecting her child, a mother tends to become over-protective, sometimes even possessive. How does one actually draw the line where protecting ends and over-protecting or being possessive begins?

Moving towards motherhood brings a fear of the upcoming new responsibilities mixed with the excitement of moving towards a new stage of completion in life. All of this converges to the point of experiencing her little one – a live doll, especially hand crafted by the Creator for her in her arms. The bewilderment she experiences seeing the miracle of nature, so eternal and yet so unique each time, numbs her to her own emotions. As she begins taking care of the newborn and settles down in her new routine, there begins to emerge a fountain of love from her heart that gives her the energy to do anything for her child, the least of all being the round-the-clock duty she has to give, for months to come. Doing everything for the child comes naturally to her out of her love for the child. In the process however, as years pass by, it also gives rise to an expectation on her part from the child to do things her way and look at life her way.

The fine line between helping the child vs. spoon-feeding him and guiding the child vs. imposing your beliefs on him tends to blur very often.

During our childhood, while being appreciative of our parents' efforts, we all also find certain faults in their parenting. Down the line when it is our turn to become parents, we make sure not to make the same mistakes as our parents did. Actually even they were doing their best for their children, acting within their own parameters of knowledge, wisdom, judgment and resources. Similarly, despite our trying to improve upon the parenting we received, while acting as parents ourselves, there inevitably are areas we could improve upon with guidance from outside.

Often in life, we get so bogged down by the nitty-gritty of day to day routine that we start living in oblivion of the bigger purpose of life. The entire journey is really aimed at going back home, to our Creator. Parenting, as every other process we go through in life, is also meant to take us closer to our Creator. We tend to overlook this basic aspect of parenting, because we get entangled in the various emotions it brings up.

A famous Indian singer was once heard saying in an interview on TV, that the entry of his son in his life had taught him about God and strengthened his bond with Him. He said, that he used to watch his toddler play and move about the house unsteadily, allowing him to explore and even allowing minor falls, yet being alert and ready to help lest he gets hurt. In the process he somewhere realized that this is exactly the way our Creator watches over us with immense love for us, being available for us whenever we might need His help.

Even though parenting, especially motherhood, might be physically taxing initially and emotionally overwhelming throughout, we can go through all of it with much more ease and grace if we remember to include the Creator in our daily activities.

One of the intentions behind writing this book is to remind the readers that even though as parents we are the creators of our child and even though motherhood is the most divine of the earthly experiences, it is the ultimate divine force that is the common thread between the parents and the child and even in the situations they experience with each other. Looking at the situations that come up with a higher perspective might not be easy always, but it definitely does help us come out of those situations smoothly and brings peace and serenity in our lives.

When a human being acts in the role of a parent, the emotions experienced are immense because one is dealing with someone extremely dear. It is easy to get carried away by those emotions and act under their influence. At that point in time, it might not be possible for the parents to see how, in the long run, their action might actually limit the growth of their child or even of themselves. It is this aspect of human behavior that this book intends to throw light upon.

Both the parents contribute in a child's growth but the mother is usually more connected with the child right from the conception of the child. While generally the father mainly plays the role of a provider in the child's life, the mother is the nurturer. Besides providing him nourishment in the physical form, she provides him with the emotional nourishment, too. This leads her into getting more emotionally involved with the child. Therefore, although most of the things said in the book apply to both the parents, the mothers would certainly relate with all the aspects of bringing up a child covered in the book.

Contents

Preface

I Motherhood 1

II The Sacrificing Mother 7

III Child above Self 25

IV Empower your Child through Surrender 33

V Support not Crutches 49

VI Teaching : Right and Wrong 61

VII Guide and Have Confidence 79

VIII Communication 87

IX What Anger Does 109

X Comparisons 117

XI Latent Desires 131

XII Adopting Motherhood 143

XIII Conclusion 151

Chapter I

Motherhood

Being a full-time mother is one of the highest salaried jobs in my field, since the payment is pure love.
- Mildred B Vermont

Each soul is in an interminable process of evolution. In order to evolve, a soul experiences birth, life and death in the physical realm. If each soul were to experience this physical world while being in isolation, there would be very limited evolution taking place. It is through mingling with others and experiencing each other that we experience highs and lows in our lives and learn our lessons.

In order to facilitate this intermingling, the system of blood relations exists. One may or may not have friends, but one will definitely have relatives to deal with. This is not to convey that friends are not important or do not contribute to our evolution. Relatives, however, are an inescapable way of tying a human being with others. Our being born to our parents connects us with many others in the form of relatives.

It is through our contracts with others that we play out during our lifetimes that we imbibe the lessons necessary for our growth.

The Creator created all creation in the first place. He created each soul, including the ones that are in human form at present. The one who created it all could have easily created each human being independent of any other human being, each time one were to be born. In other words, it was His will that mothers be there. There is an anonymous quotation that says "God couldn't be everywhere, so He created mothers". From another perspective, God is everywhere, all the time. He gives His love to us all the time through so many forms of His – the Sun, the Moon, flowers, rivers, animals, friends, etc. Why did He create mothers then? Moreover, what was the need for one to be in the mothers' womb for nine months before one is born?

If we take a deep look at the mother-child relationship, maybe we can make an attempt at figuring out the real intention of the Creator behind creating it.

Motherhood is a gift from the divine. It places a part of divinity into the mother. That is the reason motherhood is considered superior to all other relations. It gives the mother a chance to experience pure unconditional love for her child. Mother-child is a unique relationship that begins by the child being created out of the mother's body. Keeping her child for nine months in her womb while the body of the child is still being created gives the mother a chance to experience the sublime joy of being a creator herself.

Each soul is a part of the Creator. Each soul is also a creator as it co-creates its journey along with the Creator. A soul chooses to be born as a woman when it is ready to experience the ecstasy of being this close to being the Creator. Pure unconditional love that the Creator has for us all, therefore, comes naturally to a mother for her child.

A child begins its life from its mother's womb. It gets to experience unconditional love of its mother – its creator in the physical world. This is for each one of us to understand and experience love as the basis of our being. Each one of us experiences pure unconditional love from our mother – the first one we interact with – so that we can then share and experience the same with every other person we are to interact with during the course of our lives. Thus the unconditional love of one's mother is the very first emotion every human being experiences.

The real intention of the Creator is to simply make us realize that the true essence of life is love alone.

We all are the children of the same Creator. Though across regions and nations, cultures and languages may be different, the mother everywhere, experiences the same unconditional love for her child. The same Creator's love runs through our physical bodies in the form of blood. All across the globe, we human beings experience the same kind of emotions during our lifetimes. The intention of the Creator also seems to be to enable us to realize, through the mother-child relationship, the oneness of all mankind. It seems to indicate to us not to limit our love to a limited few and to remember that the basic ingredient of life is common amongst us all, and it is love.

However, in the process of interacting with others, we do experience various negative emotions. As a mother goes about playing the divine role of motherhood while being in human form, even motherhood gets tinged with certain negative energies that are so characteristic of human nature. They creep into our lives stealthily and grow unnoticed and end up giving us only trauma. Even a mother needs to look within for her insecurities and expectations to improve upon herself and evolve in the process. That is the basic purpose of human life – to evolve; to look within and through self-realization realize the Omnipotent.

Every individual that we have in our lives serves some purpose in the evolution of our soul, including our child. The fact that the child is dependent on the parents in many ways for many years misleads one into believing that the child only receives from the parents during that phase of his life. The truth is that our child becomes the reason for our growth as well. Not only do we learn new lessons during bringing him up but often the personality that he grows up to become can help us grow as individuals if we are open to it.

Love liberates. It isn't meant to bind. Yet, if we look around us, there are few instances where we find a mother living a liberated life. Mothers are often known to be the dutiful, sacrificing beings, always keeping the child's good the highest priority in their lives. Those that don't, carry guilt for it. This entire process weighs down heavy on both, the child and the mother, and creates a lot of negative energy in their lives. This cannot be unconditional love. We need to understand and identify the areas where we unknowingly deviate from it, and create miseries for ourselves.

Chapter II

The Sacrificing Mother

Women do not have to sacrifice personhood if they are mothers. They do not have to sacrifice motherhood in order to be persons. - Elaine Heffner

The act of sacrifice involves giving up something invaluable for the sake of begetting something more precious, that may or may not be for the one sacrificing to enjoy. When we hear of freedom fighters and the army men having made the supreme sacrifice by laying down their lives for their nation, it automatically touches our hearts deeply and invokes a feeling of high regard for the patriots and the sacrifice made by them. In my childhood, I read the true story of Panna Dhai, the nursemaid of the prince Udai of Chittorgarh, who sacrificed her own son in order to save the only living heir of the kingdom she belonged to. At the time an enemy forced his way into the palace, she was the only one next to the prince who lay asleep in his princely cot. Even if she fled with the prince, she would be followed and wouldn't be able to escape the enemy for long. With only a moment available to her to make a decision, she placed her sleeping child in place of the prince in the cot and covered him in wraps. She fled with the prince, thus saving the royal heir, sacrificing her own son who the enemy mistook for the prince and killed instantly.

Sacrifice is a selfless act and brings in return something priceless, not necessarily to the one sacrificing. It is an act that commands praise and respect from one and all.

However, the so-called 'sacrifices' that we make in our day to day lives really are misnomers. They are actually indicative of the priorities we have in our lives. When we are faced with two choices that are both dear to us, but are mutually exclusive i.e. we can take only one of the two courses of action, we usually weigh which of the two serves us better and choose that one. Often, one of the two would bring us immediate happiness while the other would bring contentment in the long run. Choosing the latter is often termed as a sacrifice where as actually it is a well thought of move.

Sacrificing Rest and Entertainment

Motherhood often gets entrapped in such a dilemma of choices especially when the child is still young.

When I had been married just a few months, my husband and I were going for a movie with another family. On way to the movie hall, we stopped by at their place to pick them up. We were disappointed to know that the lady was not coming along as the couple felt that their younger child, who was less than two, wouldn't be able to sit in the dark hall for too long. While getting their older child ready for the movie, the lady remarked, "One has to make many sacrifices for the children."

It was a trivial incident. Why it still remains in my memory even more than a decade later, is because of the graveness in the tone of the lady. Of course, I knew she was doing it all with love and affection for her children and family but it did convey a martyr-like feeling. I couldn't relate with the feeling too well, and I thought, I might understand the emotion only after I became a mother myself.

Later on when I did become a mother, I realized that whether it is giving up of her peaceful night's sleep for months together or giving up going for movies and outings, it is a choice a mother naturally makes for her infant because it is the need of the hour. Bringing a child into this world is a responsibility she has agreed to shoulder and she wants to perform her role as a mother, to the best of her ability. Later on giving these choices the name of sacrifices made by her, for the child, is creating unnecessary complications in her life. If a mother believes she made certain sacrifices while bringing up her child, directly or indirectly, this certainly gets conveyed to the child over a period of time. As time passes, the mother naturally develops an expectation, to be respected and rewarded for the 'sacrifices' she made for the child, especially by the child himself. These expectations, too, get conveyed to the child who is no longer a child by then. The child is an individual, going through his own experiences, learning and maturing through them.

Receiving from parents comes naturally to us. That is the way we have been right from the time we gained consciousness about ourselves and our lives – receiving love, nourishment, guidance and support from our parents. With time we all learn to appreciate and be grateful for the same and reciprocate in the way we best can. Children carry the burden of parents' expectations arising from the sacrifices they believe they made for their children, which however, only creates complications in the relationship. Expectations fulfilled often go unnoticed and those unfulfilled create blame and anguish within us. Expectations, therefore, are a sure way of creating negative energy within us.

We need to put the choices we make while bringing up our children in the right perspective. Our children are dear to us. Hence what we do for them is an indirect way of giving ourselves happiness. Having made a choice, let us take the relevant action and move on. Even if the children are unable to see that the decisions we took had them in the centre, let's not hold it against them. We did it because we wanted to. If we don't agree with a particular choice whole-heartedly, let's not opt for it. If we do, let us understand and acknowledge the reasons for the same in complete honesty.

Sacrificing Funds

Parents who have limited resources sometimes decide to use them for their children's upbringing and education rather than using them for their personal comforts. They do so in order to secure a good future for their children. It is important to understand here that though the act is commendable, they are doing so to be able to perform their role as parents in the best possible way. This act gives them the satisfaction of having done their duty well. It would be inappropriate for them to claim credit for what the child becomes or does later in his life. Not being attached to the outcome would also free them of any misery that might come their way, if the child fails to live up to their expectations. Holding on to what we did in the past and its expected outcome that we had in mind at that time, forbids us from accepting the realities that life throws up at us, which often differ in varying degrees from what we had expected. More often than not, being unable to accept the reality of the present moment leads us to misery.

Sacrifices in Career

The mother of a new-born, especially in a nuclear family, might have to give up going back to work for some time, at least till the child attains some degree of independence. This isn't easy for various reasons. The financial aspect of this choice could be a secondary issue to think about. More often than not, however, it does involve certain changes and compromises to be made in this aspect of life especially because the expenditure increases slightly due to the new arrival.

My friend Jayashree, who was a Business Management graduate and was working with a reputed organization, had to go on a sabbatical when her son was born. By the time her son was six months old, she was restless. Not being able to pursue her career made her so miserable that she actually used to curse herself for being in that situation. The magnitude of her misery was enough to engulf her heart and mind so much, that the fact that she was blessed with a healthy son and the gift of motherhood meant nothing to her.

Once a person starts earning, unfortunately the amount she earns becomes her value, even in her own mind. After that, she finds it rather demeaning being called a homemaker. We allow this discrimination in our minds even while being fully aware of the profundity of the job of raising a kid. Added to this is the insecurity that plays on her mind whether she will ever be able to put her career back on track, whether she will find a job as good as or better than the one she had prior to the baby, whether she will get her financial independence back, whether she will be able to create a social status for herself again, etc.

The break in the career can actually be traumatic for the mother as she reminisces of all the hard work she had put in while acquiring the right qualifications and then the right job for herself. Having got the desired job, one puts in mental and physical effort each day to not only maintain the job but also prove oneself worthy of and acquire timely career growth.

Taking a break from all of this means giving one's career aspiration (which for most is akin to their individual identity) a backseat. Besides, when the conditions are finally suitable for the mother to go back to her profession, she has to prove herself all over again. It also pains her to see how those who were once her peers have now become her seniors in her field, without her performance or intellect to be blamed. Yet, it would help her to remember that this was the choice she had made when she decided to become a mother. It was a duty she decided to shoulder which involves the life of another, who for some time, is completely dependent on her. Not only this, she did so because she wanted to experience the happiness that lies in there for her. She made the choice between the two ways of experiencing joy. We can think hard and take time while making a decision. Once the decision is made, we must accept it whole-heartedly. Regretting our decisions creates confusion in our lives.

An arrangement with one set of grandparents of the child to help us out during this phase or keeping a nanny could be a workable solution for us. If it isn't and if the only feasible option we have is to personally attend to the baby full time for a few years, let us not regret it later. Changes in life that will follow will be immense, but if we implement the decision with complete acceptance of the same and unconditional love not only for our child, but also our life as it is, we will be able to grow into more beautiful individuals as a result of this experience.

In modern times, the equality of men and women is a big issue. In the above mentioned situation it pinches the mother a lot when it is only her career that gets affected due to the new arrival while the father's remains more or less unaffected. This can lead her to being frustrated. The modern way of looking at husband-wife relationship, however, can work for both only if the husband and the wife both believe in it and look at their lives in parallel. Then, they can consider alternatives to solve the crisis. One alternative could be that both, the mother and the father make compromises at work, either together or alternately, till the child is independent and can start going to a play school. In countries like India, such cases would be few and to be found only in a few metropolitan cities. Similarly, there would be a few cases where the mother's position in her career would be much better than the father's in his. In such cases, it does make sense for the father to make more adjustments at work, and at home to shoulder a major part of the child's responsibility, if he so agrees to. Any of these two alternatives can be adopted, only with a mutual agreement between the couple on the issue. The decision also depends upon the fact whether the father is capable of attending to the child's needs full-time. A lot depends upon the father's inclination to do so and his upbringing – whether his mind-set accepts taking this responsibility. Even if it doesn't, getting frustrated over it is no good. A wife and her husband are together because each one serves a purpose in the other's journey. A soul chooses souls it wants to be with during a lifetime, and it has reasons to do so. Creating discord between each other due to any reason will only lead to misery. It is through unconditional acceptance of each other and of the situations we land up in, that we can find out the best way to cope with the situation. It is only later, looking back at life, that we are able see clearly how each situation came to teach us a lesson, which was so essential for our growth. Besides, in certain cases it might not be the most sensible idea to have the careers of both the parents affected.

A slightly conservative view to this situation is that the woman has been endowed with a natural sensitivity and emotional strength that gives her the flexibility to adapt to changes naturally. This appears to be the most probable reason, why in most cultures and countries it is the wife who adopts the husband's name and family and not vice versa. Even the task of bearing the child probably has been assigned to the woman considering the amount of emotional and hormonal changes one has to go through in carrying a child in the womb. Nature has given this power of adaptability to woman and chosen her to experience this unique phenomenon of being so close to being the Creator. The women who defy this concept, as something propagated, in order to allow the society to overpower the women and keep them imprisoned indoors, haven't really realized the immensity of the power they hold within.

Nine years down the line, today Jayashree is leading a happy life. She has a healthy, bright son; a loving family and a satisfying job. Being miserable earlier and leading a few years of her life in mental agony was her choice. Each new stage of life that we go through brings some unexpected situations. Calling them a problem or a blessing is a choice we make consciously.

Sacrificing Self-Esteem

A mother certainly has to spend a lot of time and energy bringing up her kids. In the initial few years, especially, she finds no time to pursue her personal interests and she makes these compromises happily. It is important, though, to break out of this new routine of doing everything for the child, as the child is growing and becoming independent bit by bit. An inertia to change or failing to recognize the need to change at this time, has the mother feeling trapped in this cycle for years to come and needlessly so. The child, of course, knows no other way than what he is made to experience, so he also gets used to having everything served to him on a platter. It is required of the mother at this time to train the child into taking his own responsibility slowly and start focusing on herself and her needs once again. All mothers need to grow as an individual. Motherhood is just one of the many roles they are playing. Motherhood need not take away from them, their accountability for themselves. Thus wastefully spending their time and energy, making life easy for their children, develops into an expectation, for an acknowledgement from children, lack of which creates frustration in them. Thus, the mother is not only depriving herself self-development, the damage becomes twofold with the negative energy of frustration that creeps in.

To a certain extent, it is laziness on her part not to come out of the pattern once set by her, to create a new one that is more enriching for her. She subtly tries to hide behind 'Oh! I do so much for my children!' and 'Ours is such a thankless job!' If we truly value ourselves, no job that we do is thankless. It is for us to look within and see whether we really value ourselves and our work enough, or have we unnecessarily kept ourselves engrossed in following a routine that involves no creativity and that, we ourselves don't respect. Either we appreciate what we are engaged in doing or work out ways to come out of the rut.

Sacrifices of a Single Parent

In unfortunate cases where the parents are divorced, bringing up children alone can be a herculean task, especially for the mother. In some cases the mother even decides not to remarry, lest her children have to suffer an indifferent treatment from the new father. This also at times is seen as a sacrifice made by the mother for the children. It is a hard way chosen by her, no doubt, for the sake of her children where she gave more importance to their well being, than to her own comforts. Nevertheless, it is unfair on her part to indulge in self-pity later, for having sacrificed her life for her children. Not only does it create a lot of negative energy within her, it also puts a lot of pressure on the children to try and make up for what she did for them, and cater to her needs of company and support, in her later years of life. The children would anyway do their best for their mother out of their love and respect for her. Having to do it, to pay for the sacrifice she made for them, is an undesirable settling of accounts, brought into a relationship that otherwise consists only of mutual love and compassion. When we make choices in our lives, the reasons should be our own, coming from within us and not from anyone else's perspective. What is right for someone else might not be right for us, and vice versa. It is unreasonable to hold anyone else responsible for the consequence of our choice.

Unplanned Child

In some cases, the 'sacrifice' bug attacks the mother when she delivers an unplanned child.

Pallavi was shocked to realize that just two months into her marriage, she was pregnant. She had wanted to enjoy her married life and freedom for some time before getting into the tedious routine of feeding the baby, changing diapers and tending to the various other needs of the baby round the clock. More than her, her two elder sisters were shocked by this news. They scorned her for her immature handling of her life. This further created a sense of shame in Pallavi.

As time moved on, Pallavi did everything to nurture herself during the pregnancy and to raise the baby well. However, through it all, an underlying sense of making a huge sacrifice of her happiness and freedom for the sake of the child was always there.

When this happens with working women, they feel their career has taken a backseat and thus their entire life is ruined because they delivered a baby when they were not ready for it.

There are instances in our lives, when we are not given a chance to make a choice. These are the times when a higher force is guiding the events in our lives. There is a karmic connection our soul has with other souls that is carried out in the physical realm through relationships and associations and each of these serves us in a big way. Our parents, siblings, spouse, children and all others we are close to, are souls we have attracted in our lives because we have had associations with them from the past, that are yet to go through completion. This is a part of the destiny we have created for ourselves. At our conscious level we might not be able to appreciate all this fully, but we must remember that after all our physical being is just a tool that serves our soul in the process of its evolution. All that is being played out in our lives has been planned out by our higher self, already. Our sensibility lies in being able to accept what is happening and taking the right decision in each moment so as to make the best out of each situation.

Pallavi's son has grown up, pursuing his higher education in the field of Commerce. She has everything in her life that a woman could ask for. Yet she goes into bouts of severe depression time and again. It is a medical condition she is prone to and needs medical help to be able to live a normal life. It is not the material things that really bring happiness to the heart. It is our attitude towards life that makes a whole lot of difference to the kind of life we live. We could have a tendency to label every unexpected situation as a problem or we could unconditionally accept whatever life brings before us, and turn it into an opportunity to enjoy life, in a way we had not planned earlier.

If we choose to resist the natural flow of life and lack the drive to do whatever is required to make the most out of what we have, we lead ourselves into feeling victimized by destiny. Thus pitying ourselves further attracts situations that give us a reason to pity ourselves and the vicious circle keeps us from enjoying our lives.

Chapter III

Child above Self

You, yourself, as much as anybody in the entire universe, deserve your love and affection. - Buddha

Child is a creation of the Creator that has been designed to lead the mother into the deception of being its real Creator. When we create something, however big or small, be it a beautifully designed home, a business, a painting, a poem or even a piece of embroidery – its beauty incessantly gives us pleasure as well as a sense of achievement. We experience a similar emotion as we watch our child grow each moment into a beautiful human being. We actually start living afresh once again, this time through the child. The carefree childhood and the innocence that we have so often missed and craved for as adults, seems alive again in front of us in the form of our child.

The Creator has meticulously designed, for us to be fully trapped in the deception by giving the child some features, habits and mannerisms from one or both of his parents. Not only this, the human child has been made so dependent on the parents for the initial few years that they actually start believing they are the Creator or God for the child. So they start showering upon the child all their love, in all possible ways. It is interesting to note that we would never have loved ourselves the same way. We are ever ready to find faults within ourselves, criticize ourselves and hold ourselves responsible for everything that goes wrong around us. We have been carrying an age-old erroneous belief, that self-love is akin to selfishness. Hence unconditional love and acceptance of the self is a concept alien to most of us. The absence of self-love is compensated by showering our child with love, for the child apparently is our creation and yet separate from us. So we not only allow ourselves this luxury without any guilt, we often go overboard doing it. In a way secretly we are doing it for ourselves, to fill the vacuum we have created inside us, by never being able to love ourselves fully and unconditionally.

Our child is a soul, on his own journey. We are together for a short span through our very long individual journeys, because we have on-going associations with each other that need completion.

Our love for each other forms the basis for continuation of this association and gives us a reason for doing things for each other, thus enabling us to carry out the contracts that we have with each other. Ultimately, our life serves only our own soul's evolution. It might appear that whatever we did for our children finally created their destiny and enabled them to become what they finally did. Actually, this is an illusion we create for ourselves and derive a sense of achievement through it. The child's soul is who created his destiny. The parents are just the facilitators. Of course, the parents' efforts and their timely constructive decisions do contribute to the child's success but all that is a part of the roles we have agreed to play in each other's lives.

Love Yourself

A mother has to be watchful of her infant's growing needs each day and in the process her life slowly starts revolving around her children completely. Since looking after her kids is an activity a mother innately enjoys, she fails to realize that soon there would be a time when the kids won't need her around them all the time. The need, by then, has actually shifted to the mother, of being around her children. The children won't have their lives centered about the mother, as she has hers about them. They have their own lives to live, in the outside world. Self-pity and a feeling of worthlessness are probable consequences a mother faces in such situations, which further lead to frustration in her. Besides, foregoing her own needs for rest, nutrition and entertainment, in the process of catering to those of her children on a priority basis, she slowly starts deriving gratification from the fact that she keeps her children's needs above her own and considers it a reason to be proud of.

Our responsibility towards ourselves should be first and foremost for us. When we give ourselves love and acceptance, it becomes natural for us to share it with everyone around us. By keeping ourselves aware of our own growth, we automatically facilitate others around us to evolve. As we evolve and shift to higher frequencies, the energy around us changes and enables those living in that energy, to grow. Thus, by attending to her own needs for growth, the mother automatically provides to her child an environment conducive to his growth. Besides, self-development is our best contribution to the universe and a tribute to the Creator, who created us with His unconditional love. Motherhood is just another role we play, maybe multiple times, during our journey.

You are Worthy too

I have known Mrs. and Mr. Dixit since my childhood. I have yet to see more dedicated parents than them. Their daughters are ever grateful to God for the blessing they have in their lives in the form of their parents. All the ambitions of the couple have always been associated with their daughters. Within their means, they gave their daughters the best they could, in terms of education, comforts and emotional support during all stages of their lives. They themselves have lived a life full of struggle always, yet every time they prayed to God, their focus was on health, happiness and success for their daughters.

While it is gratifying to see glimpses of the Creator's endless, unconditional love through this set of parents, I have often wished Mrs. and Mr. Dixit gave as much importance to themselves too. Asking the Creator for something for themselves was difficult for them as they believed in finding contentment in whatever had been already given to them. If their children were happy, it brought them supreme satisfaction and happiness. They probably failed to realize that actually they, too, were indirectly asking for their own happiness, as that lay in that of their children. The Creator's universe isn't limited in abundance of any sort. If we ask for our own lives to be smooth and stress-free along with asking for happiness for our children, the Creator would be willing to give it to us, without holding it against us.

If we could accept ourselves, our needs, and that we do deserve to be happy, we would pray for our own happiness directly. That would bring our children happiness, too, for that is a pre-requisite to our own happiness. Strange as it may sound, very often we don't believe we deserve happiness, again because of our critical attitude towards ourselves. When we do have positive beliefs about ourselves and our own worth, there is more conviction in what we are asking for from the Creator. Then our prayers are answered faster.

During the emergency instructions that are given in an aircraft at the beginning of any flight, mothers with young children are always advised to wear the oxygen mask first, in case of an emergency, before helping their children with the same. The reason is very scientific. Supposing in the process of helping her child the mother herself lapses into unconsciousness, how will she ever be able to save her child or herself?

The same principle applies to the bigger picture in life. In order to be able to help those we love, we have to understand the need to take care of ourselves first. So, keeping the child above self only generates a martyr-like feeling within, which isn't positive. We love our children, but let's make sure we love ourselves enough, too.

Chapter IV

Empower your Child through Surrender

The greatness of man's power is the measure of his surrender. - William Booth

As parents, we always want the best for our child, in every aspect of life. We want to give him the best upbringing, by providing him with the best of everything that is required for his developing into a perfect human being. That is what we want him to be – perfect in every way. We begin our efforts at doing so, right from the day the child is born and start planning his future. This process of providing the best to the child soon engulfs us so much that we assume the role of the creator of our child's destiny in our own minds, failing to see the fact that the child is an individual soul who has created his own destiny even before he came to us during his current lifetime. His journey is all about himself and his relationship with the Creator, just like ours is about us and our relationship with the Creator. We believe that since we are his parents, we know what is best for him. This is true, but to a certain extent. Being his parents, it is a part of our duty towards him, to apply our wisdom in providing him the best guidance at each step in his life. Having done our duty by being the providers, we need to release the child from our clasp of insecurity for him. For this we need to have complete faith in the Creator, who loves our child just as we do, has limitless resources, while we have limited and is forever there for our child.

The process, in a way, can be likened to that of flying a kite. Each time we pull the string, it is to guide the kite up. In order to allow the kite to actually rise high, though, we need to release it by carefully loosening our grip over the string that connects us with the kite, even if it means allowing more distance between us and the kite. We have to trust the mutual interaction between the kite and the breeze, to do the best for the kite, in taking it higher. More the length of string we release, the higher the kite is able to soar.

Throughout the process, a constant vigil is required to see when we might need to pull the string a little, in order to steer the kite in the right direction. Whether the kite actually takes the direction we had intended for it, or a different one, can be found out only after we have allowed the kite to ascend. Our job then will only be to enjoy watching the kite dance, as it proclaims its victory over the skies.

Similarly, surrendering our child to the Creator is a delicate combination of providing guidance and support whenever required while allowing the child to communicate with the cosmic energy at a fundamental level to facilitate his growth in all aspects of life.

Ownership of the Child

We often meet young mothers who can't stop talking about their infant or toddler. A child is a bundle of joy for everyone, especially for the parents, but it can be a pain for others to keep listening to a mother talk only about her child every time they meet her.

Friends had started avoiding Anu if they saw her in the market or around the housing complex. Her son was one and a half and was naturally learning a new thing each day during that phase of growth. Her friends were now getting tired of having to listen to her talking non-stop about her son's daily adventures. It was naturally a very exciting phase in Anu's life to see her first child grow and her life had begun to revolve around her son alone. Her thoughts were full of him and she had numerous stories about him, to share. This was indicative of her growing obsession for her child. This obsession later leads a mother to becoming possessive about her child, especially as the child grows up to be a youthful, dependable, helpful one around.

A child is an individual being and soon develops an independent existence of his own in this world. We can possess objects, not human beings. Helping the child in so many ways become an individual being leads the mother into developing a feeling of owning her child. This leads to problems in letting go of the child, when he has grown up, particularly when the children start sharing their lives with their spouses. This is especially so in the case of sons. While bringing up a daughter, parents usually do so, with an awareness of the fact that one day she would leave her parental home and have a family of her own. The acceptance of this fact makes it easy for them to let her go. It is interesting to note that post-marriage, usually daughters share a better relationship with their parents than sons do. The attitude of surrender in relationships, therefore, doesn't cause detachment. In fact, it allows us to experience pure love and compassion in relationships, minus all the negative energy that insecurity and undue expectations create. The latter often emerge as a result of lack of surrender.

In countries where the concept of joint families still exists and is prevalent, undercurrents of cold war exist between mothers-in-law and daughters-in-law that sometimes take the form of huge rifts in families making many lives miserable. A mother's reluctance in accepting her daughter-in-law as an important person in her son's life is the main reason behind these miseries. This lack of acceptance is what gives the mother and all others in the family so much suffering. The child, once he has grown up, deserves to be respected as an individual being. The parents need to constantly remind themselves of this and train themselves to respect him as an individual being, throughout the process of bringing him up.

When we are able to surrender our children to the Creator, we are neither shirking our responsibilities for them, nor putting our bond with them at risk. We are simply allowing the boundless divine energies to provide for and support our child in ways that we, in our physical limitations, might not be able to do. A lot of that divine support will be effortlessly provided to them, through us. It will ensure that everything that happens to them is in their best possible interest and everyone that comes into their lives, is supportive in the course of their journey. The positive energy thus generated in their lives will only strengthen their bond with us.

Nutrition Worries

A common complaint mothers have with their young children is that the child doesn't eat well. They are concerned about their child's nutrition and want to see their child full and content all the time.

Feeding the child every two-three hours even as he is growing up never allows the child to experience hunger. It is only when we are hungry that we really enjoy food. Being fed all the time without feeling the need for it himself, the child is unable to fully enjoy what he is being fed. This way he is not able to even realize the value of food and is likely to develop an aversion for it, since he is always being presented with something he never feels the need for. It is a fact that a growing child needs to be fed frequently. At the same time, the child's digestive system and his metabolism need to be given enough time to work up an appetite for him in the absence of which the child won't be able to digest the food in the most efficient way.

The universe is full of abundance for each one of us. Our child in the physical realm appears dependent on us and it is our duty to feed him when he is hungry. Yet, he is an individual who is constantly sending out vibrations to the universe to attract all that he needs. He will always get what he needs/wants.

Living in an Unsafe World

We all experience and understand that the current times are not very safe in general. One has to be on a constant guard against unfriendly elements. As we move towards the Golden Age on the planet, a multitude of negative forces have surfaced. It is by bringing them to the surface that the divine forces can put them to an end. It is like the scum that surfaces when we boil sugar in water, which is ready to be removed from the top so that what we get is sugar solution devoid of all the impurities. This process of cleansing our planet by the universal forces, however, will take some time. Till then, we have to bear these negativities around us.

Yet, the world is not full of negative forces alone. What we experience in our lives depends a lot on the beliefs and thoughts we carry within us. Our mental focus on the unsafe conditions in the environment will actually attract situations that are unsafe for us. Our fear of being faced with an unfriendly element will have us constantly thinking about it. Through our thoughts, we will continue to give energy to what we don't want to experience. Thus we will be sending out vibrations to create a situation around us to experience what we feared all along.

I am reminded of a small incident from my childhood. During a family vacation, we visited the Taj Mahal at Agra. From there we carried back a miniature replica of the monument, made in white translucent marble. I was enticed by the sight of the illuminated mini Taj Mahal that the salesman had shown us by plugging it in, and couldn't wait to reach home to see it that way again. I could have done it in the presence of my parents, but sometimes the fears of a 6-7 year old can be unreasonable. As I was plugging in the curio, while my parents were away, somehow what kept haunting me was the thought, 'What if I drop it by mistake?' The fear probably was of my parents coming to know of what I was doing in their absence and the only way they would get to know was if I had harmed the object in any way. It so happened, that the moment I put the plug in the socket, I felt a minor electric shock and I dropped the object and saw the beautifully carved and crafted piece break into pieces instantly.

A relatively insignificant incident, but it stayed in

my memory and I often wondered how or why it had happened. As I grew up, the only sense I could make out of it was that, my intense fear as I was doing the activity actually invited the mishap.

Therefore, always fearing the worst that might happen with our child, when he goes out of the house, amounts to approaching the universe with complete distrust. It is a law of the universe, that what goes around comes around, be it material things or the subtle vibrations emanating from us. Therefore, the vibrations of insecurity will only bring back to us, situations that will reinforce the feelings of being amidst a completely unsafe world. Believing in our own worthiness for experiencing the good that is there in the world around us and having complete faith in the Creator, who provides us with all that we believe in, will enable us to actually draw towards us, happy experiences throughout our lifetime. It is with this conviction that we need to surrender our child into the Creator's safe and loving hands, knowing our child will be taken care of in the best possible way, everywhere.

Trying and being with our children each time they

step out of the house or not allowing them to go for picnics and excursions with their friends limits their growth. It not only makes them dependent on the parents but also takes away from them many opportunities to learn. Even as adults when we travel or go out and meet people, we learn so much each time. Interacting with and dealing with others always gives us opportunities to learn and grow. Hardships toughen up the child and he becomes more equipped to make his way through the world. Besides, always trying to protect the child from the outside world, also teaches the child to approach the world with similar lack of trust and lack of confidence.

This is not to undermine the need to ensure the child's safety. One needs to apply one's discernment in the kind and amount of freedom to be given to one's child. Besides, all measures must be taken to make the child capable of protecting himself if any such need ever arises. Communicating with the child about certain unpleasant truths of the physical reality is necessary in order to prevent the child from suffering due to ignorance. Even providing physical training for the purpose makes sense. However, all this should be aimed at making the child fearless. It shouldn't be done with a focus on the ills of the society that one is preparing the child against.

Child in Distress

When a school-going child goes for a 3-4 day trip arranged by the school, the mothers can't help calling up their child or the accompanying teacher every day. They are anxious throughout the time their child is away. This comes from lack of trust: lack of trust in the teachers who are travelling with the children, and in the universe to take care of the child in the best possible manner. When we are able to trust and have faith in the universe, we actually allow the universe to bring our child's way the best help and the best resources for him at any time that he needs them. By believing that only we can do the best for them, we send out vibrations to limit the universe in helping them.

Children often have issues with class-mates or school-mates. This is a part of the learning process that they are in. We all have learnt a lot dealing with others at all stages in life. When our child is perturbed due to someone at school, we sometimes forget that it is a part of the child's growth too. When a mother chooses to go to the school and either talk to the other child or complain to a teacher regarding this, she is actually delaying the growth of her child in some aspect. Being an unconditional support to the child doesn't mean fighting their battles for them. Knowing that there is someone who loves and supports him unconditionally gives the child the strength he needs to face his challenges. Pitying him at any time, however, will only dis-empower him. Trusting the Creator to take care of our child where-ever he is not only relieves us of the stress but also facilitates the child's happiness.

Keeping our awareness on surrender is especially helpful during the time when our child is in distress due to any reason. At such times, all the mother wants is to see her child relieved at any cost. She is willing to do whatever might be necessary in order to have her child feeling better.

Whether the child is sick or is emotionally upset, it often makes the mother upset, to see her child uncomfortable. She even tries to give the child her own energy in an effort to provide relief to her child. These efforts from the mother, for her child, not only continue to uselessly drain the mother's energy long after the child has become normal, they actually even harm the child. The mother's energy being drained to the child creates an extra baggage around the child that interferes in the communication between the child's own energies and the universal energies, which in fact is vital for the child's growth and progress. Besides, this is the reason that soon after a child recovers from a major illness or shock, some form or ailment or physical discomfort is often experienced by the mother.

The all-pervading creative energy force can do the best for our child, only if we allow it to. Again, if what the Creator receives from us are the vibrations of 'I must do everything to help my child', He lovingly lets us do so. Only if we trust Him completely and are able to surrender our child and our wish to see him completely out of his misery, will He be able to move the energies of the universe in order to ensure the child's well being in the best possible way. This doesn't eliminate the need for the parents to do their best. Being ready to do absolutely all that is required of them is a part of their responsibility for the child. Surrendering to the Creator with an unfaltering faith in

Him and knowing that only the best possible will be the outcome, not only brings us out of a difficult situation in the best possible manner but also preserves our health and saves us from the after effects of the trauma.

When Preeti's mom learnt about the disharmony of a serious nature in Preeti's marriage, she was shocked. Despite doing their best, Preeti or her parents couldn't save her marriage. Preeti was shattered. Her mom would cry all night for months. She cried at her helplessness. A few months later she was diagnosed with osteoporosis of a high degree.

It is at such times of helplessness that one needs to remember that even our children are living out their own karma. However bad the present moment might seem, we must believe that this is the best possible outcome for us. Accepting the present moment and surrendering our child to the Creator, while doing the best that we can for our child in the present moment, is really the best we can ever give our child.

When our soul needs to connect with other souls, it takes us close to them through mutual love.

Eventually we get completely caught up in the drama of the physical reality forgetting that we are actually playing small roles in the very long journeys of our souls. We simply need to understand our duty, perform it to the best of our capability and be ready to accept the outcome, whatever it may be. Our child is always perfect as he is and our definition of 'perfection' might not necessarily be the same as that of his soul.

Chapter V

Support not Crutches

A mother is not a person to lean on, but a person to make leaning unnecessary. - Dorothy Canfield Fisher

A new born baby is so dependent on the parents for everything that it can't even turn over on the bed on his own. As the mother takes care of the newborn's minute-to-minute needs, she finds her reward in her infant's growth, which is really fast in the initial few months. As the child is learning a new basic skill every few days and outgrowing his clothes every few months, the mother delightfully occupies herself feeding, cleaning, bathing and protecting him. In fact, she had been supporting the baby within herself completely, from the day of his conception.

As the baby learns to sit, stand and walk, the mother besides being overwhelmed by all these feats of the child, somewhere down the line starts believing that the more she supports her child, the more he will learn and grow up to be a smarter person. Unaware, she develops a habit of providing everything to her child. She even believes that it is only because of all that she is doing for the child, that he is growing up to be the adorable smart kid that he is.

The importance of support from the parents for a child can't be undermined. Research has proven that abundant parental support during childhood leads to relatively good mental and physical health throughout adulthood. It also affects an individual's self-esteem and family relationships positively. There is a need, however, to be aware of the changing needs of a growing child and change the type and extent of support extended to a child by his parents, so that the support doesn't become crutches for the child that he later finds it difficult to move on in life without.

Parents provide support to help the child grow better. A mother makes all the efforts necessary to provide everything that she can to her child, only to make her child's life as comfortable as she can and so that the child can use his energies elsewhere in the process of growing and learning. This way the child is being denied the experience of doing a lot of things that he can do himself. This actually impedes his growth, instead of fostering it. Doing new things is a way to grow. The first time you do a new thing it is usually difficult. In sparing the child that difficulty, the mother is actually delaying the child's growth in certain areas. Each new activity that we learn and do stimulates our brain. Ignorantly, in an effort to give her child an easy life and spare him some hardships, the mother actually denies him experiences that will train and prepare his brain to explore and master his world better in the future.

Allowing the child to, in fact encouraging him to do little chores around the house has multiple benefits. Not only does the mother find some additional moments free to spend and interact with the child, it also introduces the child to the concept of taking responsibility and prepares him for the next stage of his life. It provides him a sense of belonging towards the family and the household and introduces him to teamwork, as he makes his contribution to running the household.

Organized Space- Organized Life

Tidying up the area, around oneself, be it a room, a table or a house, is hardly ever found to be an enjoyable activity by anyone. One does it only because one realizes the necessity to do so. A child undoubtedly is too young to realize the need for doing such an uninteresting job. However, its importance is too huge to be ignored.

Having the space around us neat and organized helps us in multiple ways. As we clear the clutter from the physical surroundings we work/study/live in, we convey to the negative energies that might be lurking around us, waiting to seep into our environment that they are unwelcome in our space. It naturally attracts positive energy towards us. Besides, by keeping our physical space free of clutter we facilitate our inner negativity to leave us and get energized with fresh life force, available to us in the universe around us. Thirdly, when we develop the habit of keeping the space around us organized, it becomes natural for us to live our lives in a more organized and productive manner. Mothers are often found clearing up their children's room/desk of its mess after they have spent time playing/studying there. The reason is not just the ever-growing love of the mother for her child that makes her to do everything that would make the child's life easy and luxurious, but also the resistance on her part to get it done by the child himself. This can usually be more taxing than the effort involved in doing it herself as the child never wants to do it himself. If the mother, however, realizes what she would really give her child by helping him inculcate this healthy habit, she would naturally find the energy within herself to do so.

Rushed Mornings

Another daily activity that needs attention, and in most cases needs to be corrected too, is that of getting ready in the mornings to go to school. Having had to go to school early in the morning everyday throughout her childhood and not particularly liked doing so always gives rise to a feeling of sympathy in the mother's heart for her child when he has to do the same day after day. So she tries to do as much as she can for him, to comfort him, by helping him with things like last minute polishing of shoes, packing the school bag with the lunch box and water bottle and thrusting a sandwich in the child's hands as he rushes out to catch the school bus. All this doesn't constitute an ideal way to start a day.

Each morning is like beginning life afresh. Thus by giving her child a rushed morning every day, the mother is contributing to the child's lack of understanding, about the significance of time. It is of utmost importance to have young children going to bed strictly on time at night, so that not only do they have a good night's sleep, but also can get up a few minutes early in the mornings, to be able to get ready in a relaxed, organized manner.

Each such healthy habit contributes multifold in helping the child grow up to be a healthy, intelligent and successful person. Having a good night's sleep every night ensures proper physical and mental growth for the child – physical growth because it is during sleep that the cell division and renewal in the body takes place more actively and mental growth because it gives his mind relaxation and rest, enough to be active and alert to face the challenges of the next day. Getting ready for school in an organized and relaxed way keeps his energies in balance, so that he not only attracts more positive situations towards him, but also is more capable of responding to them with a balanced mind in a positive manner. Consequently, the learning he receives from each situation is better and more positive. Last but certainly not the least he naturally learns the skill of time management and about being punctual, which goes a long way in contributing to his success even later in life.

Environmental Cares

Similarly, allowing the child to throw his things around once he is back from school and relax while having his lunch before the TV while someone else clears it up around him on the pretext that he has had a tiring day at school sends him signals that it is alright to take his home and mother for granted. It is through learning to respect and care for our immediate environment that we develop the sensitivity to extend a similar concern and effort for the society and the world we live in. This not only makes us better human beings, but also gives us a better environment to live in.

How a child leads his life as a grown-up has its

roots in what he has observed around him through his childhood and in the habits he has developed as a child.

Developing each little good habit is an effort initially. Huge effort is involved in making the child understand the logic behind doing a particular thing, when the child would rather spend that time playing, and then actually helping him develop that habit to contribute to a healthy growth of the child. It will save the mother a lot of time which she can devote to her personal growth which is as important, if not more, as the child's.

Evoke Responsible Behaviour

Many mothers are seen taking complete responsibility of the child's studies at home. This is a need in the beginning when the child is new to studies but need not continue as the child grows up to be more independent.

Rohini sitting down with both her children every evening with all their text books and notebooks is a daily scene in their house. She is so paranoid about her children being up-to-date with everything in each subject they are being taught at school that it actually is, with time, making her hypertensive and leading her to frequent migraine attacks. The kids certainly have the potential to do very well at academics, but she wants to leave no stone unturned, in making sure that they stand out as best amongst their peers. All this stems from her concern to do her best so that her children become the best. The point that she is missing out in this daily exercise is that surrounded by this high level of anxiety and insecurity, kids only wait everyday for the moment when their ordeal for the evening is over. Their focus is on getting done with it, not on doing it the best possible way.

Planning out the child's daily study-schedule subject by subject and actually sitting down with the child making sure he does it all as planned by her, is spoon feeding him when he can feed himself if allowed to do so. This process conveys to the child that there is someone taking care of the job so he need not bother himself with it. In fact, it never gives him the opportunity to realize that it is his job actually. This never allows him to learn to take responsibility for his own studies and he develops a callous attitude towards them. This puts the mother into a vicious circle where the more she tries to bring his attention towards his studies more is the aversion he develops for the same. This process somewhere misses the point in time when he could have developed the sense of responsibility for learning and performing well at school. Constantly being forced into something he has been trying to avoid makes a big monster out of studies instead of making him realize the purpose of the same. Again the mother is drawn into doing something day after day that she hates to but has to because otherwise the child just might not be able to even pass his exams.

The process of teaching the child to understand and carry out his responsibilities involves a lot of conscious effort. It involves developing within oneself a lot of trust in our child. What goes around comes around. This universal law holds in this situation too. When we treat someone with distrust, over time it invites un-trustworthy behavior from that person. Similarly, dealing with our child with trust and confidence in him brings forth from him a behavior that is worthy of trust and confidence. Besides, a child needs a progressive training in realizing and owning up his responsibilities and can't be expected to become completely independent overnight. Even with the responsible children, their parents need to be available to them for any kind of help they might need any time. This support is very crucial for their growth.

Mothers are seen nearing a nervous breakdown when the school exams are approaching and the child refuses to show any concern about preparing for the same. In such situations sometimes a tough action could be necessary where the child be allowed to experience the result of his actions. This can be tough but spoon-feeding him year after year to somehow have him pass the exams does him no good in the long run, either. This should ideally be a gradual process involving increasing the amount of responsibility the child shoulders bit by bit where he learns to take responsibility of his actions, too.

Rohini, while spending her energies in doing her best for her children in her own way, is not only ruining her health because of the stress she carries all the time, but is also creating an aversion for studies in her children. For them, study time is stress time. Actually her children can be their best only if they are allowed to bloom in a stress-free environment where they can actually enjoy each activity that they do. It is not by being amongst the best students in class alone, that they can be the best. Working at meeting with the parents' expectations, prevents them from even realizing what the true purpose of studying is.

As a child is growing up, he always finds his mother around ready with whatever he needs, at times even before he has asked for it. The mother starts enjoying being looked up to by the child for this. Sometimes this creates a need within the mother to have the child dependent on her, for at that stage she is unable to see that the bond between the two of them is much deeper and stronger than its current apparent form. She, therefore, is unable to see that if she habituates him with being presented with a fully baked cake, each time he is hungry, along with the icing of her love, he is going to be at a complete loss when one day he would need to bake the cake all by himself.

Chapter VI

Teaching Right and Wrong

Mama was my greatest teacher, a teacher of compassion, love and fearlessness. - Stevie Wonder

A child receives the maximum amount of love and attention from the mother. Therefore he looks up to her the most and learns a lot from her. One's mother is known to be one's first teacher. She, therefore, plays an important role in helping the child shape up his personality.

Opinions vary about the right time to start teaching a child what is right for him and what isn't. I have an interesting unforgettable experience in this regard. When my daughter was two and a half months old, we had to move into a duplex apartment, where our bedroom and the kitchen were on different floors. With my husband off to work during the daytime, I used to be left alone at home to manage my infant, the kitchen and the entire household. Still recovering from a difficult c-section delivery, I used to find it difficult to carry my child downstairs each time I needed to go to the kitchen, which used to invite screams and howls from her as she would panic each time she sensed she was alone in the room. Once, before going down to the kitchen to prepare a feed for her, I told my four month old not to panic and cry as I was just going down to get her some milk. I was amazed to realize that in that particular instance she actually waited quietly and patiently in her cot for me to return to her. Naturally, that became a routine for me – explaining to my infant that she was going to be alone only for a few minutes so she needn't panic. This was a very big lesson for me.

It made me believe in the story of Abhimanyu from the great Indian epic Mahabharata that I heard since my childhood days. It is said that Abhimanyu, the son of the great warrior Arjun, one of the Pandavas, learnt the intricacies of warfare while he was still in his mother's womb. He learnt how to enter a trap called Chakravyuh from his father who used to explain it to the mother. This became apparent when he had to actually enter a Chakravyuh created by the enemy, for the only other one who knew how to, was his father Arjun, who was away that day. He had not been taught the same ever after his birth. If a child is capable of learning so much while still unborn, he certainly is capable of learning much more after birth.

The above experience of mine taught me to always explain to my child, why I expected her to behave in a certain manner or do a certain thing. It has always worked positively both for me and my daughter.

The innocent look on a child's face is hardly a measure of the level of his potential to understand. Our children are more intelligent than we imagine and reasoning out with them always elicits a reasonable behavior from them.

Another incident that has stayed in my memory is one that I witnessed about ten years back. A group of families including mine, all friends, had gathered at a friend's place for a Sunday lunch. Everyone was enjoying a warm winter afternoon when one of the ladies present there suddenly realized that her two and a half year old son was not to be seen around. All of us present there looked for him all over the house and panic started gripping us, especially the parents of the missing child. We started wondering what to do next, while also looking for him outside the house. There was an open piece of land next to the house where a few stray dogs were roaming around. Suddenly one of us spotted the missing child playing happily near the dogs and rushed to get him home. Having got back her son safe, the obviously relieved mother got busy with her son and the group normally. I was quite shocked to see that she made no efforts at explaining to the child that it was wrong for him to leave the house alone, like he did. I couldn't help asking her about it and very decisively she replied that he was too young for that. She said that it was only after he was at least five years old that explaining him things would make any sense.

This is such a wrong assumption that elders make about kids. In fact, by five he would have already learnt so much, which is probably not appropriate for him that teaching him a different behavior/attitude would require the extra effort, of making him unlearn the earlier one. In the process, the mother and child would lose a lot of time and energy, which can be used to learn so much more. Thus, by not telling him that it was unsafe for him to go out of the house alone, she actually taught her son that it was alright for him to do so.

Never too Early

It is this lack of timely instructions from the parents to their young ones that make some of them the spoilt brats that they become. Young children carry an aura around them that is very refreshing for everyone. That is the reason children naturally attract love and adulation from everyone around them. Yet when kids display an ill-mannered and rude behavior, as some of them do, no one appreciates it even though one might not be rude enough to let one's dislike be apparent in a social gathering.

Rashmi is a teacher in a school. Her son is two and half. Every time anyone meets her, she remains occupied with her son throughout. Her son dictates to her what she should do, decides when and where she should sit or stand etc. and she complies. That is her way of showering her love on her child, but usually others get completely put off by the whole scenario, when in a few minutes they realize that all they can do while being with her is watch the mother go about following the son's commands. The child, obviously, gets insecure when in the company of new people and fearing losing his mother's attention, is making sure he gets it all to himself. In fact, he is a brilliant kid and knows how to get his way around. Only it is unfortunate that not only this behavior of his causes others to feel awkward and left out, but he is also learning that it is alright to ignore others when in their company. Without meaning to and without even realizing it, Rashmi is encouraging her son's behavior that shows lack of respect for others. Parents of bright children need to be extra careful in parenting. They have to observe the child's behavior and try and think ahead of them. It is never too early to start talking sensibly to the child. They can't show that they understand, but they do. If the child is told well in advance where his parents are taking him or in whose company they are about to spend time and what is the appropriate way to behave with them, the child will be reasonably well behaved. The social interaction will turn out to be a delight for all involved.

Young children, who exhibit no restraint in their behavior when amongst people, have parents who believe it is impossible to make little children understand the concepts of behaving well in public. Allowing a child to explore his world unrestrained in order to have him bloom to his maximum potential, also requires defining and following certain guidelines that give the process a more positive and constructive shape. Well mannered children always draw an appreciation from everyone around them, which works as a booster for their development.

Carrot-and-Stick

Another way of inculcating a desired behavior in children is the carrot-and-stick method. If the child is rewarded for having behaved in a particular manner and punished for having done the reverse, it does train him to behave in a certain required manner, but this training is devoid of real learning and constructive growth for him. When a child does something because he understands how good it is for him, it becomes effortless for him to learn and the habit also stays with him forever. This certainly requires an added amount of effort and patience on the parents' part, but interestingly even the parents would find it the natural way of teaching, once they realize how it benefits the child. Doing something for the sake of getting an external reward at the end, deprives the child of the pleasure of being passionately engaged in the activity. His mind will be constantly focused on the reward he is doing it for. He will fail to learn from the moment. He will never know the pleasure of a job well done. Putting one's best in whatever one has taken up to do, is a lesson that, if learnt early in childhood, goes a long way in defining the personal success later on. It is important for the child to learn that if he does the best that he can, the result will automatically be the best. The ultimate objective for anyone to do anything, could be the result that he aspires for, but if the focus is on the job at hand, the process of doing the job will give a lot of experience, knowledge and wisdom which can be attained only by being present in the moment. Instead of teaching them to 'expect' a reward, they should be taught to 'know' that what they will get, will be the best possible result that their efforts can fetch them. This gives the child the confidence that he has the potential to get whatever he wants. When we work earnestly at something, we get the appropriate rewards naturally.

Allowing their 'Right' to be Different from Ours

What we consider right depends on which stage of life we are in, the situation we are in, the experiences we have had and the knowledge we have acquired. Our child is an individual in his own journey. He has created a destiny for himself to experience, even before he came to us. Our job as his parents is to provide him the right guidance and support in his initial years, till he becomes physically and mentally independent which is when his own destiny starts playing a predominant role in his life. Parents can guide the child only according to their own thought process. The child might not be able to adopt everything that his parents teach him because his own thought process might not be in tune with theirs in certain aspects. The parents can still try and convince him with their logic and reasoning but after a point, it is best to allow the child to take up and live his own individual identity.

It is said that the great Indian actor Amitabh Bachchan had little interest in studies in his younger days. His father had had a lot of formal education and placed a lot of emphasis on academics for his children. If Amitabh were to follow his father's footsteps, he could never have become the legendry persona that he is today.

It is a fact that not every child differing in opinion and interests with his parents goes on to become a celebrity. Yet, each individual has his own unique path in life to follow. While teaching our children what is right and wrong, we need to also make sure that we are facilitating our child to discover his own unique path.

When the child finds his parents domineering with their ideologies which he can't bring himself to agree with, he turns rebellious. Forcing things on our child, just because he is younger to us and has been brought into this world by us, is completely useless, actually harmful. Our child has come into the world through us, not because of us. There was no way we could have prevented his coming into this world. His personality will largely be determined by the experiences his soul has had and the lessons it has learnt already. Having done our best, it is best to accept the child as he is, even if he does not turn out to be exactly how we had wanted him to.

As parents we still have to provide all the guidance and support that we can because that is our responsibility towards him and that is what he has come to us for, as our child. By trying to force our will on him, however, we only make it difficult for him to move forward smoothly on the path he has chosen for himself. It delays his evolution and creates misery for him which, in turn, creates misery for us, as his parents. Our child deserves the liberty of being an individual self, finding his own identity and moving onto his own unique path of progress.

No to Tantrums

Sometimes the parents' skills and patience are put to test when their child starts throwing tantrums. To get their way, they might start howling, screaming, hitting, kicking or even throw themselves down on the floor. The very first time when a child and the mother disagree on something, and the child gets into a rebellious behavior to assert himself, is the crucial time to convey to the child that such a behavior from him is unacceptable. During such an episode if the mother gives in to the child's demand either to stop the child from behaving in that embarrassing way or for any other reason, it immediately gives the child a signal that not only it is an acceptable behavior but is actually a technique to get what one wants.

The mother's reason for giving in to such a behavior could be one of many. She might have done it because there were other people present there and the child's behavior was causing her embarrassment. In such a case, it is important that she talks to the child later about the incident and what she thought about the behavior he had resorted to. It, of course, would help to make the child understand why the mother disagreed with the child in the first place.

Another probable reason is that the mother's need to see her child happy, overpowers her reason for which she is denying the child what he wants. This will definitely encourage the child to develop a habit of throwing tantrums for everything that he wants and his demands could get more and more unreasonable.

Sometimes it is the guilt, some working mothers carry, of not being able to give enough time to their child. Seeing their child so desperate for something prompts them to immediately give in, to even those demands that are not in his best interest.

At times it could just be the lack of energy on the part of the parents to explain to the child and argue with him why his wish can/should not be fulfilled.

Whatever be the reason, once such a behavior is given in to, it reinforces that behavior in the child's mind as a positive one because it got him whatever he wanted. The child keeps getting more and more stubborn and unreasonable. With time even the parents, having become used to their child's tantrums, start taking it as his normal behavior. The reasoning capacity of his brain needs to be triggered by the parents' conscious efforts. He can be made to understand why his behavior is unreasonable and why certain demands of his can't be met. With some effort, the parents can always find an appropriate way of conveying their message to the child clear and strong. At such times, they have to believe in and exercise the authority they have over their child as his parents in order to give him the right guidance.

Healthy Eating Habits

In the process of growing up, as we go through various health-related experiences and also through the knowledge we gain by reading, we begin to understand the significance of healthy eating habits. Having understood it ourselves, we just wish our child would eat all the healthy foods by choice. In most of the cases, it is not found to be so simple to achieve. Children usually tend to get attracted to fried food, aerated drinks, chocolates and candies. They find healthy food to be tasteless and boring. If the children are told from the very beginning the advantages of each new fruit and vegetable they are being introduced to, their reasoning mind finds the food item more acceptable and they accept its taste better. Telling the child simple things like carrot is good for his eyes and sweet lime keeps the viral fever away during changing weather actually draws the child to carrot and sweet lime as these two enter his psyche like two heroes who work for his good.

Besides, children learn more from what they see around them than from what they are told. If the others in the family happily eat fruits and vegetables every day, those are what the child will learn to eat and enjoy. If anyone in the family regularly creates a fuss over food, the child is sure to pick up that trait. For example, if a parent often mentions his fear for a particular subject like Mathematics or Chemistry in front of his child, the child is likely to develop a similar fear of/dislike for the same subject. It is, therefore, important to watch our words and conduct when our young ones are around.

If every time the family is celebrating, the child is allowed to have his favorite food that doesn't qualify to be a healthy food item, say a pizza or a pastry, it creates an association in his mind between pizza/pastry and happiness or freedom. Naturally then the child would crave for a pizza or a pastry more often for everyone really craves for happy moments. When the child is under stress, he craves for these 'happiness giving' foods even more. This craving for junk food is reinforced in the child when every time the parents feel like pampering him they treat him to the junk food of his choice. This is what leads some children to being addicted to junk food. This is not to say the children should never be allowed to have such food items. Moderation needs to be exercised, though. More regularly a child is fed a certain type of food, more he develops a taste for the same.

Similarly, in his early years when the child shows a lack of interest in eating, the mother finds it easy to feed him by having him watch television while she feeds him. This begins as a convenience for the mother as she can easily keep feeding the child who gets engrossed in watching the show on the TV and doesn't protest to being fed as that would create a disturbance in his own entertainment. In the process, however, the child gets addicted to watching TV while having his meals. The mother now finds it objectionable as the child, instead of focusing on the food he is eating, has all his attention only on the show he is watching. Food is known to benefit us more if we have our awareness on the food we are eating.

While bringing up children, one has to be very cautious as to what one teaches the child not just by what one says but also by what one doesn't say and by what one does. Children learn a lot by observing. For this reason, one has to be careful about the environment the child lives in. When we encourage our child through appreciation, we teach him to be sensitive to others efforts. When we ignore the child at a time when he needs our attention, due to being pre-occupied for some reason, we teach him to be self-centered and insensitive to others.

Children learn the art of expressing themselves in the process of growing up. Initially, it is not possible for them at their age to understand and express how what they are receiving is affecting them. It is up to the parents to understand their needs and provide as much positive inputs to them, as they can, because that certainly affects their learning process positively.

It pays to believe in your children. Believing in

them as they are still growing up, gives them the confidence they need and has the potential to produce miracles through them.

Chapter VII

Guide and Have Confidence

You must understand that seeing is believing, but also know that believing is seeing. - Denis Waitley

The purpose of relationships in life is to experience the joy of loving and of being loved through them, while on the journey of evolution. Love is not meant to bind, it actually liberates. Having loved ones around provides the support one needs time to time in the process of moving forward on one's path. The responsibilities we have towards each other are merely temporary roles we have agreed to play in each others' lives. Getting too bogged down by them makes us lose the right perspective on them.

Our responsibility of guiding our children and teaching them the best way to experience this world is meant to bring out the best in them. That is possible only when the parents realize that it is a role of facilitators that they are playing in the lives of their children. They can't really decide the outcome of their efforts in terms of the child's personality. It requires a lot of patience on the part of the parents to provide the child with the knowledge that they possess and then allow the child to respond to it, as he best can and at the speed that comes naturally to him. Based on the child's response, the parents can take a decision about the further inputs they need to provide in terms of training/guiding him themselves, or taking professional help for him. After all these efforts, all they have to do is watch the child bloom into a beautiful individual that each one naturally is.

Have Confidence

When parents teach their child to walk, they allow the child to walk on his own. They don't accompany the child everywhere that he goes just to see that he is taking each step correctly. They have the confidence, that having learnt it once, he will be able to walk on his own. However, while being around him they are able to notice if there are any flaws in his gait and do whatever is required to amend them. They need to have a similar confidence in the child's capabilities in other areas as well. Once they have provided basic guidance, they ought to set the child free to find his way through the world. This liberation for the child liberates the parents as well. Yet, this liberation comes at a price. It requires the parents to be alert always, and watch out when the child might need an intervention from them, in order to enhance his performance or even correct him where he might be going wrong. They need to be available for their child any time he might need them, while allowing him to find his independence at the same time.

Fourteen year old Arpita finds her life extremely boring and a drag. After she goes home from school, her parents expect her to spend the rest of the day in front of her books, studying. She is allowed no other activity as they believe that studying hard and scoring good marks is what will ultimately make her successful in life. While the role of academics in life can't be underestimated, the need for rest and entertainment is as significant, as this is what will allow the knowledge acquired to be imbibed and assimilated. Even if Arpita sits in front of her books all day long to keep her parents happy, it is unlikely that she actually studies all that while. This is not only making her develop an aversion for academics, but is also killing the sense of responsibility in her.

Trust makes Trustworthy

Parents of teenagers sometimes feel insecure about their children hanging out with others of their age group. They are afraid of them getting into bad company and being exposed to bad habits. While being vigilant about our children, the company they keep and the places they frequent, is a responsibility we must diligently carry out, trusting them teaches them to be trustworthy. Not being able to trust them amounts to lack of trust in our own parenting process. Let's raise them such that we can trust them. This calls for introspecting whether we truly trust ourselves and the nurturing we have provided them. Maybe a change deep within us will transform the way we are raising our children which, in turn, will reflect positively in their personality.

Guidance to the children from their parents is

meant to trigger their growth in the right direction as opposed to imposing their own beliefs on them.

It is observed that each generation that comes into this world is different from the previous one. Technologies have advanced in various fields and newer techniques and ideologies have found their way into the lives of people. For example, people of my generation first started using the internet much after they had turned adults, where as our children were introduced to the same while they were still in primary school. Not only this, they seem to pick up the new technology much faster than us. They certainly cannot be expected to blindly believe in and follow what we have believed since our childhood times.

Having grown up in a small town, I was always taught by my mother to never answer back, whatever be the situation. As my daughter was growing up, I was happy to see that I was doing a good job of passing down my values to her as I never found her being rude with her elders. However, I got a jolt one day when I realized the conflict she was experiencing within. With a look of annoyance on her face, she asked me whether I meant to convey that even if she knew what an elder was saying was wrong, she was expected to follow it instead of voicing her opinion. I was taken aback. I couldn't tell her to follow advice and do something that she knew was wrong, as I had taught her to do what she truly believed in. I tried explaining to her how important it was to respect the elders for their age and benefit from their experience. At the same time, I had to agree that my young one had a point.

Rearing children involves guiding their behavior without overly restricting the same. Allowing them their spontaneity ensures their growth beyond our perception.

Having emphasized the importance of allowing the child to have his independence and the need to have him realize his responsibilities, it is important to point out that the duty of the parents is to provide an atmosphere conducive to learning and growing. For example, provide the child with an atmosphere at home that is appropriate for him to be able to study in peace, advise him about the need and advantages of studying and doing well at school and even be there for him when he needs your help. You certainly can't do the studying part for him and any attempt at doing so will only prove counter-productive.

Unconditional Acceptance builds Confidence

The mother of a class-mate of my daughter, when she was in class six, would come to school to collect notebooks from her son's classmates herself when he would miss the school for some reason. She would even send a written note for her son's teacher, if she would find that her son deserves to get half a mark more in a particular class-test. It was a known fact that she used to do a lot of writing work for her son at home, so that he would be left with enough time to prepare for his tests and exams. She was keen that he always topped in all his exams.

This behavior of hers was a reflection of a deep sense of insecurity she carried for her son. If she believed in her son, she would trust him to do all that is required of him to study and perform well. She was clearly conveying to her son that anything less than the top rank was unacceptable to her. The kind of support she was providing her son was keeping him from realizing what it is to be independent. Not only this, her son would be extremely miserable in class every time anyone in class scored even a mark more than him in any subject. He was imbibing this lack of self-acceptance. His mother's insecurity was clearly being passed on to him, as all he seemed to be concerned about at school was his exam scores. The purpose of getting good scores at school was thus being defeated as the personality and self-confidence of the child were actually getting ruined in the process.

It is your confidence in your child that will give him the impetus to perform. Remember your child has an agenda to fulfill in his current lifetime. Lack of confidence in him will pass on to him your vibes of insecurity. Let him know that you are always there for him, whenever he might need you. Your confidence in him will bring out the best in him.

Chapter VIII

Communication

Seek first to understand, then to be understood.
- Stephen Covey

Communication is known to be the heart of any relationship. A parent-child relationship forms the basis for a lot that the child experiences later in life. The parent is forever connected with the child, no matter how grown up and independent the child might be. The experiences of the child as a grown up, therefore, affect the parent as well. Thus, any parent-child relationship is very important for both, the child as well as the parent.

The communication between the mother and the child begins from the day the child takes birth as she responds to each and every need of her child, by providing him with what he needs. Even though the only way the baby can communicate is by crying, she can identify what the baby needs each time. In this process the child develops a trust in his mother and starts recognizing her, as someone he is completely secure with. During this stage, there is a lot of non-verbal communication that goes on between the two.

Communication with an Infant

When my daughter was still an infant, every time I had some additional work on hand e.g. packing to be done for an upcoming trip or extra cooking to be done for guests, I would desperately wait for her to go to sleep so I could attend to these jobs. Often, at such times I would find her more restless than usual and it would be quite impossible to put her to sleep. It took me a while to realize that it was my own anxiety that would make her restless at such times.

Just like a baby receives, understands and recognizes the mother's love through her touch and her subtle vibrations, her anxieties also similarly get conveyed to the baby inadvertently. Unknowingly, the mother communicates to the child that she is restless herself. Sensing the disturbance, the child becomes insecure as he finds his sole source of comfort distraught.

By being anxious about the pending jobs we are causing stress to ourselves and conveying the same to the child as well, and making the situation even more difficult. It would be a good idea to bring our awareness to remaining peaceful. Anxiety about the work to be done may be inevitable, but it actually acts as a hindrance in completing the work in the best possible way. Mentally trying to get a job done, while trying to attend to the baby, prevents us from doing justice to either of the two jobs.

Besides, how a mother goes about handling her life conveys a lot to the growing child. The child doesn't judge what he sees. He just learns from whatever he sees in his environment. If he observes his mother managing her daily activities peacefully and in an organized manner, that's what he learns to do. If the child gets to see his mother spending a lot of time before the TV or on phone, that is what we find him doing soon. Children watch their parents' behavior with others and grow up to be a replica of their parents in many aspects. Therefore, it is essential to watch ourselves from the day our child comes into our lives. If we want our children to have certain values, it is necessary to lead them by example. Expecting them to do something, opposite of the behavior we ourselves exhibit confuses the child and leads us to a situation where the child stops listening to us and is labeled stubborn.

Dual Standards

In our day to day lives, in order to avoid certain situations that we fear, we sometimes resort to some insignificant, harmless lies. For example, if we get late while leaving for a dinner party at a friend's place, we blame the delay on a traffic jam.

We underestimate our child's intelligence, thinking he is too young to understand what we are up to. The fact is that the child observes everything that is happening around him and develops beliefs from each observation. Watching his parents lie can harm him in multiple ways. He is still too young to judge whether the lie was harmless, but not too young to pick up that lying is acceptable. Lying, we all know, is bad because it harms one's self-confidence. One lie leads to another. Each one weighs somewhere on the conscience and ultimately affects one's belief in oneself adversely. Slowly the person loses trust in himself, resulting in lack of trust in everyone else, which in turn, would attract untrustworthy people and unpleasant situations. Besides, by blaming our delay on the traffic jam, we are also teaching the child to blame other people and situations for our actions. Taking responsibility for our actions empowers us to correct them, while passing the blame onto others dis-empowers us, as we get drawn into the vicious circle of blame and guilt.

We want our children to imbibe the virtue of honesty. We expect them to be honest with us, to begin with. At the same time, mothers are often seen feeding their reluctant children by distracting their attention. Parents often make promises to their children in order to evoke a certain behavior from them, which are not kept once the critical moment is over. This inconsistency in our speech and actions makes the child lose faith in us and soon brings us to a stage when the child stops listening to us. It is a common sight where parents keep telling their children not to do a particular thing, but are clearly ineffective in amending the child's behavior. This can be very frustrating for the parents as the child's behavior makes them feel inadequate and ineffective. They fail to realize though, how they, themselves are responsible for landing in such a situation.

The actions of the children are childish, but their minds are forever grasping and learning. Their skills in self-expression are still developing so they are not always able to express themselves completely and accurately. Underestimating their minds on the basis of their looks, actions and speech would make us give wrong stimuli to their ever-receptive minds. If we always say what we mean and vice versa, we will be able to build our credibility with them. This credibility comes handy when we want to pass on to them, the knowledge we have attained through our experiences, without them having to learn it the hard way. For us to be effective in parenting, we must be careful, and say only the things we mean and make promises that we mean to keep. This helps them to trust us and our words and knowledge.

Turning a Deaf Ear

It is also necessary to refrain from being repetitive in giving our advices and instructions to the children. Parents repeat themselves because they are saying what they truly believe in and want the child to understand and follow it. However, as we repeat ourselves frequently, the child uses his own tactics to be physically present and even give physical expressions of listening, but tune off internally.

It was around the age of 10 when my daughter started going to the nearby market on her own to buy the stationery items she needed regularly for school. I had given her enough practical demonstrations of crossing the road carefully, before finding the courage to let her go on the road alone. Yet every time she would leave home to buy her stuff, I would make it a point to tell her to look on both sides of the road, wait if a vehicle is approaching from a distance, never to run while crossing, etc. After a few times, I could sense she is getting irritated but I continued with the ritual. Perhaps I was doing it to cover up my guilt of not accompanying her each time she went out. Once on a similar occasion as she was leaving to buy some chart paper for a collage she had to make and submit in school, I started off...."Be careful while crossing the road. Don't be in a hurry. Watch out for the traffic in both directions and please get me a loaf of bread from the market." When she returned, without the loaf of bread and also insisted that I had never mentioned it, it struck me that she was tuning off each time I was repeating the monotonous set of instructions. I learnt my lesson to trust my child to have imbibed my instructions after a point. I was glad the lesson came to me easily, without having to see her miss something significant or crucial.

Turning a deaf ear to our words is a kind of a defense mechanism for the child to save herself from the irritation and frustration of having to listen to the same thing repeatedly.

Confrontation vs Unconditional Love

Sometimes, during parenting, we directly or indirectly come to know of an act of our child that we disapprove of. This gives rise to a need for us to confront the child on the issue. We are not able to accept the fact that our child could do something that is against our principles or morals and want to get an account of the same from him, so that we can reprimand him for the same. Knowledge of that act of our child has probably let us down because we *expect* our child to follow the morals we believe in. Since we fear things going out of our control, we intend to bring about an instantaneous correction. The problem gets compounded when, realizing that he has committed a mistake and is likely to be punished/scolded for the same, the child lies about the incident. This aggravates our anger which makes us lose control over the situation completely. Seeing the situation out of our control, we lash out at the child, resorting to the means of force to try and correct the situation. In the process, we miss out the fact that there obviously had been some reason for the child to behave in a manner that he did. Without addressing those reasons, the problem cannot be eliminated from the root. Forcing the child to act differently in future only creates complications in the child's personality.

It would be interesting to observe that the unconditional love and acceptance for our child that we boast of flies out of the window the moment we feel let down by an act of his, only because he failed our expectations.

Rohit works as a manager in a reputed bank in a small town. To provide the best education for his daughter, he sent her to a college in a big city, even though it put him in a tight spot financially for four years. One year after she had started studying there, a friend of Rohit told him that he had seen Rohit's daughter with a guy and that the two seemed to be in a relationship. Rohit, having made compromises in his own life for the sake of providing the best for his daughter, naturally expected his daughter to keep her focus on studies in order to make the most of the time, effort and resources . The news of likely deviation of her interests gave him such a shock, that he immediately wanted to confront her. Even if the news he had received was true, it was possible that the girl was anyway doing justice to her studies. The fear of our children not meeting our expectations can make us insecure enough to instantly lose faith in our children. If we approach our children with a lack of trust in them, it puts them on the defensive. Then they will do anything, including lying, in order to get their parents' love and acceptance back. On the other hand, conveying our unconditional love and acceptance for them puts them at ease and they are more likely to unfold the realities of their life before us.

Our child craves for our acceptance and approval. He always tries his best to do things that will fetch him these. At the same time, there are innumerable factors that govern his behavior – the experiences he has with others (fellow students as well as teachers) at school, our behavior with him, the beliefs held within his subconscious that are not so active in his childhood but start playing their role as he is growing up, etc. The moment he realizes that we are confronting him for something that he probably shouldn't have done, his fear of losing his parents' acceptance and approval can naturally provoke him to lie. Therefore, it is of utmost importance in such situations that the child be first reassured that he is unconditionally precious to his parents and that they accept him as he is, always. This requires the parents to introspect to see what makes them not accept their child as he is, unconditionally.

Calling a certain behavior of the child wrong is hugely different from calling the child wrong, especially when seen from the child's perspective. When we call the child wrong, we immediately send him vibrations of being unacceptable. In response to this, the child would either get the feeling of being unacceptable (and hence of not being loved) which would lead to deterioration of his self-confidence and self-esteem, or would retaliate by shutting himself off to whatever we want to convey to him. For him, it is equivalent to being attacked. On the other hand when we point out a certain wrong behavior of his, he finds it more acceptable as he doesn't find himself being rejected then. Then he is more likely to be willing to listen to our point of view and consider bringing about a change in his behavior.

An interaction with the child based on these grounds would enable the parents to figure out the wrong input that the child has received, that prompted him to act the way he did. Instead of expecting an instantaneous change of behavior on the child's part, it would work well to identify and bring about changes in those aspects of the child's life that are providing him the wrong stimulus.

Two-way Channel

Sometimes the image that a child portrays at home is different from the one he does at school. If we hear from someone about a quality of our child that we are not familiar with, it usually is a challenge to accept it especially if the quality being talked about is negative. We believe that since we have raised our child from day one, we know him inside out. As such, it is completely unacceptable for us if someone tells us anything negative about our child that we ourselves are not aware of. Such a situation usually happens when at least one of the parents have a tendency to dominate over the child. With a father who is a strict disciplinarian or a mother who is extremely particular about the child's daily study routine, the child would live in a constant fear at home. He might keep certain aspects of his true self hidden from them, fearing harshness or rejection from them.

Parent-child communication is often seen as a channel that the parents use to convey their guidance, morals, knowledge etc. to the child. Any communication channel, however, works best only when it is open and free both ways. It is when the baby cries that the mother feeds him or changes his diaper. However, as the child is growing up and starts responding to our verbal communication, we tend to forget to keep the other side of the channel open. The parents' minds get shrouded with their need to teach their children new things and telling them what is right and what is not. In fact, what becomes increasingly important as the child is growing up, having his own experiences away from us and developing new thought patterns, is to be open to receiving what he has to convey to us or ask us. Communication is possible only if the child feels the parents' willingness to listen.

When he tells us about his experiences and his opinions on various things, it tells us a lot about the stage of his inner growth. In fact, if we pay attention to the child's narratives, sometimes one sentence or one phrase can shock us, as we realize how deep his thoughts are or how mature his analyses are becoming. This knowledge gives us cues as to what guidance we need to give him at various stages. Even simply being listened to and paid attention to boosts his self-confidence and improves his self-expression. Yet it is a fruitful exercise only if we can lend him our ear without judging him as he passionately narrates his experiences. Any advice that we might have for him can wait. His need at that particular moment is to share his emotions.

Timely Attention

Sometimes when our child asks questions, we might be pre-occupied or lacking the energy to answer and explain. Yet, not answering the child's queries, will either with time suppress the natural curiosity that each child has that enables him to learn and grow, or will make him seek his answers elsewhere. The knowledge he then receives could be something we don't approve of. It is best to either answer them or lead him to a proper source of knowledge like good books, encyclopedias, internet etc. under our guidance, when he is at an appropriate age. Ignoring the child's queries because the parent is pre-occupied or upset, can also give the child a feeling of being unloved. If such a thing happens often, it can affect the child's personality adversely.

Timing the Corrections

Another place we need to exert restraint in criticizing/correcting is when the child is making an attempt at something new. This brings forth my memories of an experience from my daughter's childhood. We had stayed in a small town called Chhindwara during the first four and a half years of her life. It is a beautiful place with very affectionate people, in central India. My daughter went to an English medium school there but the language of communication in general was Hindi. She just knew a few words of English when we moved to Bangalore, in south India. The regional language there was Kannada, which we didn't know. People there were not conversant in Hindi. The only option, therefore, was to communicate in English, which almost everyone there knew. So my daughter also started picking up English. My husband and I were helping her do so by speaking only English with her, at home. One day as she got onto the stool especially kept in the bathroom for her, in order to reach the wash basin, she called out, “Mamma, tap is the tight.” It brought a smile on my lips and I was about to correct her, when instinctively I didn’t and just gently helped her open the tap. What the child needs at such times is acceptance of his efforts and encouragement rather than criticism.

It also reminds me of the time when I was doing the MCA course in Patiala and was staying in a hostel. Many of the girls in the hostel were from Punjab and spoke Punjabi often. When I first tried to speak with them in Punjabi, all of them laughed aloud. I knew the correct words but couldn’t get the right accent and they found it funny hearing me speak their language in an odd way. Even though it was all in fun and I knew no one had meant to hurt me, I could never gather the courage to speak in Punjabi in front of anyone. It was also because Hindi and English were both commonly used languages there. Since I knew them both, there was no pressure to learn Punjabi. Yet when I remember the incident, I realize that even as a discerning adult, the response I received to one of my first attempts at something new, affected me deeply.

Having made this point, it is essential to point out, that it is nevertheless a responsibility of the parents to correct the child's behavior whenever they feel the need to do so. If we get over-protective of our child, not pointing out his mistakes, lest we hurt him, they will soon become a habit with him. He could be ridiculed outside home, which will be more difficult for him to handle. Sometimes it is best to stay silent in the heat of the moment, but we as parents have to identify and use the most appropriate times to get across certain important points to the child. That will help him improve himself.

Therefore, every care should be taken to do things that keep the communication channel between us and our children open. While appreciation improves their self-confidence, punishment crushes the same. While we teach them to value themselves and others by giving them attention when they seek it, putting their queries off can create a sense of worthlessness in them.

Peer Pressure

Each decade has a different flavor in terms of music, cinema, hair-dos, clothes etc. This impacts the young generation of any decade the most. They are still discovering themselves and developing their personalities. Their parents have already found their own styles. Since the parents have been through their own cycle of understanding the environment and grasping what they found appropriate for themselves, they tend to believe they must share their understanding with their children. The fact is, however, that the parents had got more influenced by their peers in their youth, especially when it came to the external appearances and certain aspects of their behavior than by their family members. The same holds true for the new generation now. When they move outside the house, their need is to appear like one of those they mingle with, and not an odd one out. This comes from their need for approval in the society. It is only after one has found acceptance in the society that, one usually proceeds to discover and enhance one's unique characteristics and start reveling in one's individuality and originality.

In this entire process, what the youngsters need at home is a lot of acceptance and patience while they are still establishing their identity in the society.

Vigil is important here. In this process of seeking acceptance from friends, the youngsters fall into the trap of addictions like smoking and drinking.

Communication with the child, coming from trust, helps more than that coming from suspicion, fear and insecurity. Trusting them and accepting them unconditionally while keeping our channels of communication open with them gives them the confidence they need to deal with the outer world.

The peer influence is not always bad, even if the parents might often feel it is. It also brings out certain beautiful aspects of a child's personality. In an effort to leave a mark on those around, he learns to use his wit, charm and knowledge in an effective manner.

Research has shown that peers and community play a huge role in shaping up one's personality. This is more so in times of rapid change. By trying to control this factor in our child's growth, we might be actually harming the child more than protecting him. As parents we want to impart the lessons we have learnt the hard way. In doing so we aim at developing clones of ourselves, when our children have their own destiny to discover, enhance and experience; which is most certainly very different from ours.

A parent-child relationship continuously goes through changes as the child grows up but it requires a conscious effort on the part of the parents to keep changing their ways of communicating with their child based on the child's age and the stage he is, in his life. By the time the child becomes an adult, even though he still needs guidance and support from his parents, he makes his own decisions. Too much guidance from the parents can appear to him as their interference in his life. It is by following his own instincts and leading his life appropriate to him that he can best discover his own unique path. The parents, at this stage, have to understand the significance of providing him support by silently being by his side. Watching him grow in his life through his own decisions and applauding each big and small success of his, continues to strengthen his confidence in himself. There comes a stage in every child's life when the parents should start refraining from giving him their advice and help till it is sought. Sadly, most mothers fail to realize when their child reaches this stage, and live in the illusion that they will always know better. They are unable to let go of the hold they enjoyed over the child's life. This can be suffocating for the relationship between the two.

Any relationship between any two individuals grows stronger only with constant nurturing through love and care. The moment we take it for granted, it starts deteriorating. The same holds true for a parent-child relationship as well. To nurture this relationship, the responsibility lies more with the parents as they are older and wiser. Besides, they set an example for the child to follow. Right communication is a tool that goes a long way in developing and maintaining a healthy, mutually rewarding relationship.

Chapter IX

What Anger Does

Two things a man should never be angry at: what he can help and what he cannot help. - Thomas Fuller

Most of us have experienced anger within us sometime or the other. Some of us fall prey to it more often than the rest but we all do realize that anger does more harm than good. The only good that can probably be attributed to it, is, that the energy it brings along with it is sometimes useful in getting difficult things done. The good that it does rarely matches up to the harm it causes, though.

Anger figures up many a time in the process of parenting. One reason is that the responsibilities one is shouldering in catering to the needs of the family and work (for those working outdoors, work for the day ends with the day but for home-makers it never does and, in fact, increases on the weekends) bogs one down so much that any small event that happens unplanned, or goes an unexpected way is enough to trigger a spurt of anger. Sometimes when the child is acting stubborn and refusing to act as the parent wants him to, anger is the natural outcome. Very often the parent might be infuriated due to something that does not have anything to do with the child at all, but the child just happens to be the easiest one to vent one's anger upon. If the parent, in her childhood, has been at the receiving end of her parents' anger often, it becomes a learnt behavior with her. She inadvertently tends to deal with her child with anger when it is her turn to become a parent.

Whatever be the reason, the mother usually regrets what she said or did while in rage once the anger in her has receded. Having done so repeatedly, her habit of getting angry becomes a reason for an internal conflict in her, which not only frustrates her and creates a dislike in her for herself, but she is also guilty for having been unduly harsh with her child. This slowly lands her in a vicious circle where this inner conflict gives rise to anger in her at the slightest stimulus which she later regrets. She then hates herself even more than before. This is how anger slowly becomes a deep-rooted habit with us, which seems completely beyond our control.

The harmful effects of anger are far too many to ignore. We have just seen how it has a way of finding deep roots within a person and ruining his peace of mind. Anger clouds one's reasoning and one completely loses control over what one is saying or doing. Often a person doesn't really mean the things he says while angry, but words being powerful as they are, have already done the harm by the time the one who said them, realizes his mistake. With children, harsh words lashed out at them in anger can cause an irreparable damage to their self-esteem as they are not at an age to understand what is happening. What goes into their ears reaches their mind and affects their psyche. Besides, it makes the parent unlikeable to the child at that time. This makes us lose our authority over the child, bit by bit. It is essential that the child holds his parents in high esteem, to really follow the guidance they provide him. It also creates a fear in the child for the parent, which in turn, closes the communication channel with the parent. This is a big loss for the parent as well as the child, because it is through an open and free channel of communication between them that their relationship thrives. It not only plays a crucial part in the child's development but also is essential for the parents who find nourishment in togetherness with and the love of their child. This is where seeds of life-long loving relationships between parents and their children are sown.

There are some parents who, in a fit of rage, even resort to physically hitting the child in desperation to assert their authority over the child. Besides hurting the child's body and scarring his tender mind, it grossly fails the purpose it was aimed at. It certainly does ascertain their authority over the child, but only of a superficial nature. It will make the child fear the parent and hence, not do something the parent disapproves of only to avoid his anger and being physically hurt. The child will, however, lose respect for the parent and want to indulge in doing things his way when he is sure the parent won't come to know of it.

Sometimes what we get to know or understand about a particular incident or behavior related to our child could be very different from the child's reality. What we understand of it might enrage us but on the basis of that if we get furious and scold the child only to realize later that the truth had been something entirely different, it would be a very sorry situation for the parent. Therefore, it is always best to not respond to any situation by way of anger. A peaceful discussion between the parents and the child, where the child is allowed to put forth his point of view can usually help resolve any matter of concern that the parents might have for their child.

Having understood so many ill-effects of communicating with our child in anger calls for an earnest effort on the part of the parents to look within and acknowledge, if anger is proving to be a problem with them.

To find a solution to any problem, it is very important to acknowledge the problem first. Once we accept that a problem exists and determine within ourselves to come out of it, we naturally shift our focus to the solution for the problem and therefore begin attracting the same. Denying that anger is a problem, we will always find others to be the reason for our anger. This will only make the problem persist.

If we look at any situation that enrages us or did

so in the past, it will reflect our feeling of being helpless in the situation, to be the cause of the outburst. When we are faced with any situation regarding our child that we had not anticipated and is not to our liking, like a bad report card, a complaint about the child from school, the child being irresponsible at home or displaying unacceptable behavior towards us or others, we suddenly feel helpless because we can't instantly reverse the situation to suit our liking. Maybe we have even tried to deal with a similar situation earlier and seem to have failed. We are unable to accept things as they are. Interestingly, as we refuse to accept the reality, the reality refuses to change. It makes us feel helpless as we feel things around us are out of our control. We don't want to accept that we are in a situation that we cannot handle. The result is getting angry at the child who seems to be the reason for that unpleasant experience of ours. This anger towards him is actually an inadvertent effort to camouflage our helplessness and ascertain our authority over the child.

Any situation that we are ever in is there in our lives for a reason, even if we had not invited it consciously. Trying to fight it only makes it persist. Being miserable due to it, can be our choice but it is there for us to experience. The best way to experience it is to first accept and acknowledge its existence. By accepting its existence, we can not only change it in our favor through our efforts, but also learn the lesson that it has in store for us. This enables us to stay calm and level-headed which equips us to find ways that will bring us out of the situation in the best possible way. The authority that we thus experience over ourselves is naturally conveyed to the child during our communication with him. Anger makes us lose control over ourselves and subtly conveys our helplessness. Dealing with the child in a peaceful, assertive manner helps to make the child see why he is expected to change his behavior. Reasoning out with the child often works better than being angry with him.

If the real reason of anger had been something other than the child, the same rule applies. It will do us good to acknowledge the situation that is making us angry, and then work on the best possible way to turn it in our favor. Allowing ourselves to vent our fury on the child not only makes us resent ourselves for the same later, but also gives a very confused signal to the child about how he is supposed to behave. In fact, if we deal with the child calmly, his innocence, love and joyful disposition eases our stress, leaving us better equipped to face the challenges in our lives.

However, sometimes a little anger becomes unavoidable while communicating with our children. It becomes a need at such times in order to convey our authority over them, and send across a message that is important for them to understand. Feeling guilty for having dealt with them with anger at such times and trying to make up for it by showering extra love and affection soon after sends only confusing signals to the child. The message that we had wanted to convey to them through our anger might then actually be lost.

Thus when we deal with situations with our awareness in the present moment and not in the expectations that we had and move forward in life with unconditional acceptance of life as it comes, we usually are able to cross all the road-blocks in the journey of life and still maintain a positive attitude.

Chapter X

Comparisons

When you are content to be simply yourself and don't compare or compete, everybody will respect you .
- Lao Tzu

Comparing ourselves with others around us, in almost every aspect of life, becomes so much a part of our nature that unknowingly we pass it on to our children as well. Society conditions us from our birth to evaluate ourselves based on others. At home siblings are often compared with each other in various aspects. At school our intelligence is judged based upon how our performance compares with that of the fellow students. At work, our performance is judged and rewarded in comparison with our peers.

We are made to believe that only by comparison, can we grow. This is not true. Through comparison we can grow only to the extent of the person whom we are being compared with, or a little more than that. Not to our own unique level. Each one of us has immense potential in our own unique areas. Comparing ourselves with others actually constricts the scope of our growth to the area someone else has the potential in. If we focus on ourselves and our growth instead of that of the others around us, we will be able to identify our own path and be able to perform to our highest potential.

Healthy Competition

We all know that competition creates immense stress. Anything that creates stress is in conflict with our basic nature of love, peace and happiness. To justify our focus on competition, however, we have coined the term 'healthy competition'. What we imply through this is an act where we don't intend to harm our competitor, but use their performance to motivate ourselves to perform better.

Yet harm it inevitably causes, to ourselves, and in multiple ways.

Energizing the Competitor

The concept of depending on another for our growth is far removed from the basic essence of human growth and development which is triggered from inside. By focusing on our competitors, their potential and their performance, we energize them. If we use the same energy to determine our goals, build confidence in ourselves and do what is required to achieve them, we will be making a more constructive use of our energies. Once we understand this, we will stop forcing our children to compete. By focusing on the achievements of our friends' children and on the peers of our children, we end up wasting our energies. It could be better utilized in ascertaining the areas of interest for our children and helping them develop their full potential. Besides, through our own behavior, we can also effortlessly teach our children to focus on their own performance, rather than on comparisons with others.

Every time test sheets would be distributed in class after the teacher had marked them, the prime question in Abhinav's mind would be whether Sonal's marks were more than his. If he would learn that she had got even half a mark less than him, he would instantly be at peace (only till it was time for another test). This knowledge would make him rejoice and demonstrate a sense of pride in his behavior. Scoring more than Sonal also meant being the top scorer in the class as hardly ever did any other student get more marks than both of them. On the other hand, scoring less than her would make him feel miserable beyond consolation. It was a common knowledge amongst his classmates that his life would be miserable at home if he failed to get the top score in class. Some parents derive a sense of pride, if their child tops the class. More than this, it is essential for the self-respect of some parents, that their child tops in academics.

Getting the top score in class isn't necessarily equivalent to being the best. Abhinav's focus was to somehow get more marks than everyone else. He was being conditioned to accept himself only if he performed better than those around him. Always focusing on being better than others, he would never be able to learn to really be his best as he would never be able to realize what his interests really are.

Doing all this out of fear of his parents, might actually make him grudge his parents later in life. Spending one's growing years under such pressure and in anxiety would keep many of the neural connections in his brain from being activated.

Let's look back at the times when we were students and try to remember what equations existed between the classmates, based on their academic performances. It can be very enlightening to realize how wrong some of those perceptions had been. Most of our classmates from those times are well-settled in their lives and doing well in their respective fields. Differences do exist in life-styles and environments but all that is a part of our karma, the destiny we have created for ourselves to experience during this lifetime. The only way to improve upon what we have created for ourselves is to take each step with awareness and positive attitude. If we practice this ourselves, we naturally teach our children to do so too. Trying to pressurize our children to perform better by giving examples of their fellow students, can only prove counter-productive to their overall growth, which is what matters in the long run.

Eating to Beat the Stress

Many children resort to compulsive eating at such times of stress. Filling up oneself with food is an attempt to make up for the lack of love and understanding the child is experiencing from the parents. At a time when he is struggling to gain an understanding of himself and his needs, he finds himself burdened with his parents' expectations which he finds overwhelming. The only ones he can fall back upon for anything he needs seem to be completely oblivious of his needs. This makes him resort to something that at least gives him a temporary comfort.

Paving Way for Jealousy

Love encourages co-operation. Competition fosters jealousy. It isn't always possible to outperform our competitor. When we find it difficult or impossible to achieve our goal of performing better than our competitor, it naturally gives rise to jealousy. We are jealous of them for effortlessly (in our perspective) having something that we are unable to get, despite our intense desire and hard work. Jealousy is a negative emotion that, if it stays unchecked, can instigate us to try and harm the competitor in an attempt to prove ourselves better than them. This, too, is against our basic nature of love. Therefore it silently creates stress within us.

If we are aware of such negative emotions as they are cropping up within us, we can eliminate them at the root by using the right approach. As parents, we would be doing our children a lot of good by teaching them to unconditionally accept others around them as they are and to focus on their own development rather than on others' performance.

Blaming the society and the education system for the wrong inputs we provide to our children, will not reduce the harm they cause. If we believe in a certain approach completely and are convinced about the reasons we should follow it, it is possible to adopt it in our lives, even if it is different from what everyone else around seems to be doing.

Unique or Duplicate

We all want our children to be able to develop their own unique talent and demonstrate it. At the same time, by pointing out to them how we expect them to perform like someone else, we give them a signal that they can easily get our love and approval by doing what someone else is doing. This becomes a goal for them to achieve. Thus by comparing our child with another we are actually motivating him to duplicate the other one's personality trait or talent.

Our growth can be a pleasure if we focus on our potential and passion. It can, on the other hand, cause us immense misery if we use others' performance as a yardstick for our growth.

The other harm this approach causes is that it generates insecurity within us. Always wondering what the competitor will do, and whether we will be able to outshine him, will make us live with a constant fear of losing out to the competitor. Fear is another strong negative emotion. Any negative emotion works only to curtail our capabilities.

It is usual for parents to feel proud when their child does well at something and experience jealousy to some extent when the other child we know excels at something, especially if they had wanted their child to excel in that particular field and he couldn't.

Imposed Expectations

It is worth noting here that this negative emotion arises because of the expectations the parents have had from their child. It is actually the need of the parents of proving to themselves or to the society. Parents invest their efforts and resources in their child and want their child, in return, to do well. Through their child's success, they want to experience contentment themselves. It is basically a fulfillment of their own desire that they are looking for through their child. It would be a blunder on their part to think that because they are putting in all their resources to facilitate the child's learning, their expectations from him will not cause him stress. If the child's own aspirations truly match those of the parents, the inputs from the parents in terms of their efforts and encouragement will prove to be beneficial for the child. The child, however, is not even given a chance most of the times to understand what his aspirations are. The journey for the child in such cases is extremely stressful.

In our need to see our child doing better than others or above a certain level, we become blind to the effect it has on the child. Feeling helpless at being unable to meet the parents' expectations, some children get drawn to taking the fatal step of trying to end their lives. Knowing very well that this is a reality that happens in the world around them all the time, parents choose to close their eyes to this probability.

When we can learn to actually unconditionally accept our child just as he is, we can begin to derive happiness from others' children success as well, rather than being miserable inside on seeing their glory.

Comparing Siblings

Any two souls choose to become siblings due to their connection with each other and their individual connection with the common set of parents. Having been born to the same set of parents and having grown up in the same environment, they go on to live their own specific karma.

Anurag, the elder brother of Neena, was an above average student while Neena shone brighter in the academics. Anurag would always be told by his parents to learn from Neena's example, do well in school. Anurag was brilliant in sports and dramatics but that never seemed to bring enough happiness to his parents. Being always negatively compared, with his sister, was slowly making him lose his self-esteem and he started resenting Neena for this. Neena experienced his resentment in their mutual interactions. Her young mind was incapable of analyzing his behavior towards her and created hatred in her for Anurag in turn.

When parents point out to a child how well his sibling is doing, the child gets afflicted by a feeling of jealousy and animosity for the sibling. The love and bonding that siblings naturally share, get tinged with enmity as one tends to blame the other for his short comings. These feelings developed in childhood go a long way in defining the child's personality as well as the mutual relationship the siblings share lifelong.

Very often the siblings of a famous personality are not so famous. That does not mean that one is any less or more than the other. We can only be our best by being our natural self.

Only with love and complete acceptance of the

child, as he is, can we bring out the best in him.

Parents vs Children

We sometimes tend to compare our children with ourselves as well. Certain events in our childhood stand out as landmark events such as getting to own a bike for the first time or having gone for a movie with friends for the first time. We tend to set standards for our children based on the age we experienced such landmark events.

We expect them not to need a bike before the age we had started using it. We expect them to continue going for outings only with their parents, as we did in our childhood. Everything is best done at an appropriate time. Yet we can't ignore the fact that the world our children are experiencing today is much different from the one we experienced in our childhood. We see the young generation these days doing so much better than their parents had done, in their youth. There was a time when one would build one's own house close to the retirement age. Today's youngsters acquire a house as one of their first assets, soon after they have started earning. Travelling abroad was a luxury only few could afford, a few decades ago. These days no vacation is considered complete without a trip overseas. Every generation notices as young parents, that their children are studying in primary school, what they studied in senior classes. We feel pity for our children being burdened but the fact is that they are actually ready for it and we all see them coping well with it.

Each generation is usually more evolved than their parents. The world that they come to is much more advanced than the one their parents had come to. In fact the parents need to be open to learning from their children at various stages.

Sometimes parents feel insecure that they would be left behind if they don't catch up with the next generation. Learning and being open to receiving new knowledge is a prime responsibility we owe to ourselves in order to continuously grow. Imbibing change in our way of thinking to keep up with the changing times also makes our children more receptive to what we have to impart to them. Yet, we don't really have to completely change our perspectives, morals and behavior simply to be able to keep pace with them. Accepting them in their kind of clothes and hair styles and understanding their need for space and freedom, will give them enough stimulus to accept us as we are and to respect our values and morals. They chose us to be their parents and they had good reasons for doing so.

The information boom through the audio and visual media and internet has exposed them to the entire world too early. It is natural for the growing mind hungry for learning, to absorb various things from there. Trying to cut them off from everything that interests them will either make them rebellious or make them an introvert who carries various complexes. Effort is required to maintain a balance between allowing them to experience the world their way and making them understand and honor the values their parents believe in. As always, reasoning out with them works wonders. One needs to be clear about one's reasons before expecting an intelligent teenager to honor them. It is only by being clear about our own identity and by respecting ourselves for what we are, that we can naturally command respect from our children.

Chapter XI

Latent Desires

Anything in life that we don't accept will simply make trouble for us until we make peace with it.
- Shakti Gawain

A major aspect of human life is fulfillment of desires. Our desires guide our thoughts and actions. A fulfilled desire leads us to a new one. From childhood till we become parents, many of our desires get manifested into reality. Those that don't lie submerged below the current priorities of the mind. As we see our child growing up, our own childhood memories and those of our youth get triggered. While reliving our childhood through our child, we allow the desires lying dormant within us to re-surface. This time we want them fulfilled through our child. Some of our desires couldn't materialize, because our parents had different aspirations for us. Since they played dominant roles in our lives then, their wishes overpowered ours in certain areas of life. When we become parents, as these unfulfilled desires of ours start re-surfacing, we easily forget the pain we went through when we weren't able to follow our dreams. We even begin to believe that it is in our child's best interests to follow that unrealized dream of ours.

Career Options

The aspirations that parents have for their child's career are often guided by either what they are successful at or what they wanted to do but couldn't manage to. For example, a doctor (especially if there is a generation of doctors in his family), would like his child to become a doctor. The reasoning is logical. The child would have generations of expertise, experience and contacts to benefit from. Similar is the case when there is a generation of lawyers in the family.

On the other hand those that couldn't, for some reason, adopt the career they had dreamed of, feel immense satisfaction in dreaming of their child taking up the same career. Since they have the authority to make decisions, they often make sure they get their way. In his heart, Satish carried a deep regret that he couldn't become an IAS officer. As his daughter Swati was growing up to be an intelligent, responsible girl, he started harboring a desire to see her enjoying the perks and charisma of being an IAS officer. Even though, unlike many other parents, he never pushed Swati too much into pursuing this career, she did feel guilty of not being able to give her father this happiness. Her interests always lay in sciences and she went on to become an engineer.

When a child is given no option but to pursue and adopt the career his parents choose for him, it may lead him to a life full of drudgery later. Sometimes the child, on growing up, decides to switch professions later in life. Having to start afresh in a new field late in life can be stressful too. Yet, if the heart and soul of the person are tuned to it, life becomes interesting. Not everyone is able to do so, though. Then one simply lives life without any enthusiasm and zeal.

Often in such cases the child isn't given a chance to even think there might be something else better for him. The child finds it extremely stressful finding his way into the profession chosen for him by his parents, but doesn't know the reason for it. Even his low performance in that field is attributed to his lack of competence, drive or dedication.

Pushing vs Facilitating

Each new generation comes into a world, with more opportunities than what his parents had been exposed to.

Mrinalini, now 40, grew up in a large joint family. She was keen on learning music and dance but her parents never considered it important enough to arrange coaching for her. When her daughter Shikha was growing up, she not only made sure Shikha learnt music and dance, but enrolled her in every possible hobby class that she could. Shikha ended up learning classical dance, music, painting, tennis, skating and various other things. By the time she reached mid-teens, she was fed up and just wanted to be free and enjoy herself during those hours of her life when she was not studying. The hobby classes were only adding to her stress levels rather than easing it out from her life.

When we step out of our childhood and youth, a

part of us is still stuck in those times. That is because we haven't truly accepted the reality. The happy memories of the past are readily accepted by us and integrated within our beings. The times when things happened against our wishes are hard to accept. This lack of acceptance makes us want to somehow change it to a desirable form whenever possible.

We have lived our lives so far in the best possible manner we knew. It is our past and exists only in our memories. As long as we refuse to accept this fact, we will continue to make ourselves miserable. When we force our wishes on our children without even realizing we are doing so, we pass on our misery to our children.

Mrinalini was sending her daughter to learn and excel at various skills also because she wanted to prove that her daughter was better than every other child around, who was learning any skill. Lack of acceptance of ourselves, as we are, translates into lack of unconditional acceptance of our child once we become parents. It is our need to see our child doing everything that any other child is doing, and better than all of them. That makes us accept our parenting better. We believe that whatever we couldn't do as children has been made up for, by making sure that our child does all that. Also this is our way of being accepted in the society through acknowledgement and appreciation.

It gives us satisfaction to think we are providing the education to our child, little realizing that we are actually burdening the child beyond his limit, that keeps education healthy for him. Shikha's brother, 9 years younger to her, was more fortunate. Mrinalini had realized the futility of her efforts with Shikha. For her son Aryan, she was more relaxed. Appreciating his interest in badminton, she allowed him to be trained by a professional. Not only is he becoming an excellent badminton player, he is also more relaxed, emotionally balanced and happier child than Shikha turned out to be.

Usually the eldest child in the family is the one to bear the brunt of the parents' latent desires. By the time they are dealing with their second child, they have either achieved some satisfaction of having done their best or have realized the harm it did to their child.

Satisfying the Ego

Any achievement of our child, besides giving us the satisfaction that he is growing up to be a bright child, gives us a sense of pride. It gives us immense happiness to be able to declare among our friends and relatives as to how well our child is doing. We use our children's achievements as a basis to seek acknowledgement for ourselves from those around us. If it is our need to be acknowledged and accepted by the world, it will manifest as a continuous need in our life. On the other hand, if we accept ourselves unconditionally, so will the world around us. We will then not be applying the subtle pressure of our need on our children. Our attitude of self-reliance will naturally be passed on to our children in the process of our bringing them up. Therefore, they will effortlessly be able to develop all those qualities and talents in themselves that will make them self-reliant.

Suniti was always anxious about her daughter Neetu as a child. Her son, who was younger of the two children, had always been a confident child and usually scored well in his exams. Neetu, on the other hand had been very unsure of herself, always passing with difficulty. Her mother's perennial anxiety about her, only added to her lack of confidence in herself. However, she was very talented in dance and arts. When the time came for Neetu to seek admission in a professional course, it was an arduous process for her and her parents. They applied for admission to many institutions. She wasn't able to get through in the first list of the college of her preference. She was keen on doing a course in fashion designing. More than anything else, Suniti was worried about facing her colleagues. The shame that Suniti felt because her daughter could not clear the exam, was passed on to Neetu as well. Luckily Neetu made it to the college of her choice in the second list. The air was suddenly cleared around Suniti. The cheer and joy was back in Suniti's life, as she could now proudly proclaim before her friends that her daughter had got admission in a reputed institute.

Desires are governed by the mind. The mind is driven by the outer world while the soul has a path of its own.

The soul that has come through us, as our child, has a definite path to follow. When the child is able to do what best suits him, he will be able to evolve. This will bring about the best in the child naturally. The path that one has to follow usually gets reflected in the child's personality, in the form of his aptitude. This might become evident very early in some, while it may take more time to show up in others. Anxiety about our child's future, however, is futile. It only works to clutter our mind and keep it from seeing what is evident.

Whose Responsibility is It

Sometimes at the parent-teacher meet held in schools, parents are seen complaining about their child to the teacher. Often mothers would complain to the teacher that the child doesn't study enough at home or doesn't listen to her. Parents waiting in queue to meet the teacher are also seen sharing amongst each other their complaints about the teacher.

Passing the blame never helps. Our child is our

responsibility rather than anybody else's. A teacher, handling 40 students in a class and meeting them for a few hours in the day has a role to play in guiding them in becoming responsible, educated human beings. It would be unfair to expect her to be responsible for how the child behaves at home. Contrary to this, the environment that the child grows up in at home plays a bigger role in directing his behavior towards his fellow students and teachers at school. Receiving certain inputs from the teacher, we can actually work at providing the right stimulus to the child, to improve and mould his personality in the right direction.

The teacher is always under pressure to have the children in her class improve. She points out the child's faults to the parents. Parents have a lot of expectations from their child and they want the teacher's help in having those met. The child, thus, is put under pressure from both ends. He is often clueless as to why no one seems to be happy with him when he is doing the best that he knows. It is the job of the parents and the teacher together to provide him with the right encouragement, in order to bring about the desired positive changes in him.

Children, when they score poorly in exams, are scared to show their result to their parents because of the likely reprimand. When a child studies simply to get marks good enough for his parents, there's little value attached to such an education.

Constantly being made to believe he isn't up to the mark in his parents' eyes, only creates an inferiority complex in him. This is either reflected in his timid, introvert behavior or he tries to camouflage it by bullying his peers and displaying rude behavior with elders.

Whatever we give in a relationship is what comes back to us. Expectations from our child make us give him signals of rejection at various times. This is what we are creating for ourselves, i.e. to receive the same thing from them in future. Providing them with nurturing and guidance while loving and accepting them unconditionally teaches them to love unconditionally too.

Chapter XII

Adopting Motherhood

Adoption is when a child grew in its mommy's heart instead of her tummy.

Human life is known to be full of sufferings and miseries. A situation that we don't like is termed as a misery. Each situation that we experience has been created by us for reasons not easy to fathom by the conscious mind. It is something the soul regards necessary to endure as a part of its growth.

When a couple is unable to have a biological offspring of their own, the reasons are attributed to the infertility of one or both of them. Actually the reason for infertility is connected to the souls.

A couple had been married for eight years and had no child. The reason was revealed in a few of their healing sessions with me as follows.

The husband, during his past lifetime, was a caretaker in an orphanage. The wife was a cook at the same place. The guy had no attachment to the kids. He was just doing his job of looking after the administration of the place. In fact he used to get irritated with the kids often. He didn't like his job much as he wasn't particularly fond of children. The cook was doing her job diligently. She had no particular attachment with the kids either but was rather happy in her job. One day the food that was prepared for the kids got poisoned. How it happened was not clear but it was clear that it was not done intentionally by anyone. Unaware, the staff of the orphanage served it to the kids. All of them got sick soon after consuming the food. The poison was so potent that despite all efforts, many of the kids couldn't be saved.

Even though the cook was not to be blamed, she developed a sense of acute guilt. All she could see was that the food made by her somehow became the reason for the suffering and death of so many innocent kids. The caretaker, too, was severely shocked by the incident. He did his best to ease the suffering of the children and prayed hard for their lives. During that hour of suffering, he was surprised to realize how connected he was with those children. Seeing them die, he felt remorse for having hated them at times. He resented himself for having been so callous towards them.

During this event, and later, the regret that both of them developed at having failed in their responsibility for the kids, found deep roots in them. They both developed beliefs of being unworthy of handling the responsibility of kids. As they shared the common grief, they developed a bond with each other at the soul level.

In their present lifetime, they got together as husband and wife but their subconscious beliefs of being unworthy at handling the responsibility of children, created a situation where they couldn't have a biological child of their own.

In another case, a couple who couldn't have a child of their own naturally, had been an affluent couple in a past lifetime. They had a son who was spendthrift and in bad company. They tried a lot to change his habits but to no avail. They started restraining the amount of cash that was made available to their son. They looked at the wealth that was at his disposal to be the main reason for all of his wrongdoings. Being rendered helpless irked the son so much, that one day he killed his parents in cold blood, so that he could have free access to all their wealth. The parents had already been feeling guilty, realizing their mistakes in the upbringing of their son. After they were murdered, the souls were miserable and developed feelings of unworthiness for bringing up a child. This sense of unworthiness did manifest in their next life as they were unable to have a biological child of their own.

Thus our soul always has its reasons for creating a situation in the current lifetime, but our conscious mind is unable to access those from the depths of our subconscious.

In cases like those mentioned above, often couples resort to adopting children in order to experience the bliss parenting has to offer. This action is triggered by a decision taken by their conscious mind.

The basic emotion experienced in the process of

parenting is unconditional love for the child. It is inherent in each one of us. It surfaces for our children right from their infancy. Even when a mother gives birth to her child, the real bond that she develops with him comes through her association and interactions with the baby.

This is not to undermine the bond that she develops with her child while she holds the baby in her womb. But if it is a part of our karma, not to experience a certain aspect of life during our current lifetime, it is best to accept it. Blaming anyone for it wouldn't really help.

It is only unconditional love that the child triggers in us. Everything else in the process of parenting is learnt. We pick up traits from our parents, from the world around us, from books and from whatever our conscious mind tells us.

Any soul that comes into our lives, including that of the child we have adopted, is amongst us because it is a part of the lesson we are in the process of learning. Parents and their adopted child also have purpose to serve in each other's journey and thus contribute to each other's evolution.

Having pointed out the similarities in parenting a child – biological or adopted, it is important to remember that in the case of adoption, the parents and the child, both carry certain insecurities deep within. The child, once he knows he has been adopted, is likely to carry the grief of being separated from his natural parents. Every time the parents' actions are against his liking, he is likely to blame it on their being his foster parents. Likewise the parents are likely to fear being misunderstood whenever they are stern with the child for his own good.

Dealing with these insecurities is also a part of the lessons to be learnt by these souls in order to grow and evolve. Insecurity is a negative emotion we can choose to breed within or refuse. Our choice will determine the kind of bond we develop with those around us. It would help if parents would address these insecurities and make the child understand the futility of such fears.

While adopting a child, both the parents ought to be in perfect harmony about the decision. Such a decision, if implemented half-heartedly even by one of the parents, can make all three lives involved miserable and completely ruin the personality of the child.

Mr. Chatterjee was a senior director in a multinational company. He was of a very generous nature, always giving away his clothes and food to the needy right from his childhood days. He had two children of his own. When he expressed his desire of adopting a third one, his wife was not keen initially. Realizing the intensity of his wish however, she relented. The motherhood in her had been satisfied bringing up her two children and she was a little indifferent towards the third child. She never felt inclined to make his favorite food or be up at late hours to look after him, when he would be up late in the nights studying for his exams. Probably she resented the additional responsibility she was never keen on taking up in the first place. This child grew up carrying a huge amount of complex in him, making his parents' and his own life miserable throughout.

This decision involves the lives of the parents as well as that of the child being adopted. In the case of Mr. Chatterjee, it was a deep desire in him to adopt a child and hence it was his need. Yet, for his wife it was something she was doing for her husband. One can make others happy only by being happy themselves.

The topic of adoption is vast and needs extra sensitivity. It deserves an entire book devoted to it. The intention of including it in this book is simply to point out that the relationship between parents and their adopted child is susceptible to the problems and issues of a normal parent-child relationship. The added complications in this particular relationship are also a part of the karma the souls have decided to live. We deal with souls that we have connections with, from the past. Our relationships with them in the current lifetime manifest so that we play out those roles now. What makes most sense is to accept the present moment as the best that it could be and move ahead in our relationships with a positive attitude.

Chapter XIII

Conclusion

There is no way to be a perfect mother, and a million ways to be a good one. - Jill Churchill

There is no formula for ideal parenting. There really is no 'ideal' mother. At the same time, each mother is the ideal for her child. Our behavior is governed by so many factors unique to each one of us. So is the way each mother brings up her child. A mother's behavior with her children is a function of the stage of evolution she is in, the karmic lessons she has learnt and her karmic connection with the children as well as with her husband. In any case, the best that anyone can do in a situation is to accept the destiny one has created for oneself and make the most out of it, while using our will in the present moment to alter the future course of our destiny and create better times for ourselves.

Life often throws up many complications at us. If our effort is at simplifying our lives rather than focusing on the complications, we are sure to find our peace of mind on the way. The web of relationships we are enmeshed in seems to drain a lot of our emotional energy. This happens because our relationship with those around us and close to us needs completion. If the soul carries guilt for someone, it might decide to pay for it by suffering at the hands of that person in some way. Yet when it creates a situation to accomplish that, we are able to see only the present. We are unable to understand that it is actually emanating from within as it is a need of our own soul to go through it. Fighting what is happening in the present, therefore, doesn't yield much. Accepting the present and applying our capabilities at improving our future is the best we can do. This holds true for the parent and child relationship, too.

It is better for us to go through our lives with a sense of detachment. Detachment here certainly doesn't mean the opposite of loving or lack of love. In fact, it is what we get by experiencing unconditional love while living in complete surrender to the Creator. Unconditional love is experienced through accepting and loving everyone and everything as it is. Surrender to the Creator comes naturally when we completely trust the Creator to take care of each one of us (including our children) in the best possible way. Then we are able to carry out our role as parents with ease and without unnecessarily complicating our lives.

Sometimes being conscious about the kind of parenting one is providing to their children makes them overly concerned in this aspect. Mothers are often seen being extremely cautious about each word they speak to their children and each emotion they express before them. This results in the mothers developing unnecessary guilt. Spontaneity in relationships strengthens the mutual bond which is vital for the child's development.

To provide our children with a childhood that gives them a firm foothold in life, we need to work on ourselves first. As we learn to really love ourselves unconditionally and trust ourselves, these qualities get reflected in our behavior with our children. We then effortlessly teach them to love and trust themselves, thus bringing up self-confident and loving human beings. Children have a huge pressure on their minds to constantly get the love and approval from their parents. As we teach them to love and accept themselves unconditionally, they stop doing things just to please others. When they live their lives experiencing self-love and acceptance, each act of theirs is filled with compassion and confidence, not insecurity.

Each individual is in one's own spiritual journey and attracts from the universe the knowledge one needs, at any given time. The required knowledge can come to us through our experience, through someone's words or through a book. It is up to each individual to be aware of this moment and be able to receive what one is being offered by the universe and keep making the best choices in each moment.

I hope we are able to recognize and acknowledge the limitless love of the Creator in our lives and around us.